The Longest Half Mile

By

Richard Lukon

The Longest Half Mile

By Rich Lukon

Cover Art by Pahl Hluchan

PREFACE

"Spirit of place! It is for this we travel, to surprise its subtlety; and where it is a strong and dominant angel, that place, seen once, abides entire in the memory with all its own accidents, its habits, its breath, its name."   - Alice Meynell

This is my coming of age story. It is the story of a boy-chameleon who changes colors to match the rock upon which he has perched. It is the story of his struggles to fit into his new coat of many colors.

Shortly after my eighteenth birthday, I left San Francisco with $25 in my pocket and worked my way around the world. The journey took three years and involved a number of adventures on three continents and several oceans.

The sailor's life provided a sense of calm, of space. Months of crossing brought shelter through isolation, a place to hibernate, a place to digest events and reflect a place to mature.

The work-a-day group of Australians that took me in allowed me freedom to purge some of my demons, to improve my survival skills. On these distant shores, I entered a world full of madness that offered new perspectives on the boundaries of human behavior.

In France, I found hope, a new identity in a gentle world. It became my haven where social order seemed a thing of beauty, where I proudly assumed the esteemed role of being a representative of *l'Amérique*.

A summer full of adventure began on a U.S. Air Force base in Madrid where my discomfort with the America lifestyle resurfaced. In Israel, I roamed the countryside from kibbutzim to Solomon's Mines entering into a caring relationship as well as dangerous situations.

Returning to France for a second year, I studied that marvelous society's literature under the microscope as I tried to reconcile the great works with my daily life. I struggled to fit into a culture which turned out to be far more complex than I had ever imagined.

NOTES FROM THE AUTHOR

Memory is a complicated thing; it is a relative of truth, but not its twin.   - Barbara Kingsolver

This memoir owes its very existence to that unique group of friends and acquaintances around whom my story, indeed my education as a young man, developed. All the people and places are real. All the events actually happened. Most of the dialog has been fabricated from memories to reflect the spirit of events or is partially reconstructed from notes in journals that I kept at the time.

I have changed some names out of respect for personal privacy. This book is more the result of recollection than historic research. Like the blind men and the elephant, all those involved were undoubtedly touched by these same events in very different ways.

If you are able to travel smoothly with me on this journey across time, it is to a large degree because of the invaluable input of Ann Thompson whose teaching and editing skills greatly enhanced the writing. Thanks also go out to all the members of my writing class whose rich feedback proved both encouraging and invaluable.

Particularly appreciated are the contributions and support of Judith Brynda, Morris Chassen, Rosel Civelli, Barbara Eggleston, Gisela Foster, Joanne Gunn, Mary Kuo, Valerie Lee, Rosalinda Oneto, Clarence Nihei, Edith Robertson, Nancy Samuels, Ann & Andy Sermersheim, Lonna Smith, Reed Stevens, and Maggie Sullivan, for their keen observations that helped to refine the presentation. Special thanks go to Ursula Smith for helping me discover the title. I am very fortunate to have benefited from Jean Gallup's proof reading skills that rendered the text more understandable.

I wish to express my appreciation for the help and support of my brother, Steve Hluchan, who provided input and advice as only a brother could. I thank Karen Hluchan for lending her editorial skills.

From the other side of the Atlantic, my dear friend Guy Foropon has refreshed my memory on more than one occasion. Presented as "Felix" in the book, Guy has remained a loyal supporter of this effort and an admired friend over these many years. He continues to live in the charming town of Cours-La-Ville near Lyon with his lovely wife Monique.

I wish to extend my deepest appreciation to Pahl Hluchan for creating the artwork that is the front cover and to Alicia Robertson for contributing to the development of overall appearance of this book.

For more information about this book including photos, updates, awards and more, see my Blog:
http://longesthalfmile.blogspot.com/

CHAPTER ONE
Leaving America

Shipping Out

Having never actually held a real handgun I turned the revolver over slowly. It felt heavier than I ever imagined. Its familiar shape pulled me back to boyhood, as I practiced my one twirl action, a fearless knee high cowboy. Black and white cowhide strapped loosely around my nine-year-old waist, I strived to perfect a simultaneous drop of those plastic Roy Rogers six shooters into their holsters.

But this pistol lay ominously in my palm. The weight of the heavy steel was closer to that of the rifle I used as a pre-teen. When we split into warring factions shooting across the ravine at enemy school boys, strategically slipping from tree to tree in a struggle to win the B B Gun Wars back in Tennessee.

The dead weight of this gun in my hand brought on dread, a cold chill that I had not felt since that night lying in the shallow ditch by the railroad tracks. My buddy Billy was holding a portable stereo. Dan clutched dollar bills in one hand, his other fist wrapped around a bunch of coins. We lay still, watching the bursts of red and whites light from police cars repeatedly swing inches above our heads and listening to the screech of sirens as they raced along the nearby streets looking for us. It wasn't the first time we had broken into that clubhouse to clean out whatever we could find. It was just that we had never thought the owner would install a burglar alarm.

No, this pistol was something else, something we only imagined. We joked about a gun as we sat on the hoods of our cars at sunset in the boulder scattered foothills of Riverside, California's high desert. How cool would it would have been to use a gun instead of someone over eighteen to get our booze. We laughed at the thought, sporadically hurling empty beer cans towards the glowing red bull's eye dropping out of sight beyond the sagebrush.

This gun scared me. It had my finger prints on it now. The Riverside City Police had taken a set of my prints that past spring when I spent the night in jail for not having enough money to pay a traffic violation. I had wanted to see what jail was like. It stunk.

The teenager who called me aside after getting off the bus looked about my age. He wore a T shirt and faded jeans. His hands were now firmly planted in the pockets of a cotton jacket. His empty stare reached out from some spiritless recess as he spoke, "It fires real strong. Twenty bucks en' it's yours."

Looking up from the gun, I recognized that blank gaze buried in an expressionless face. A face that told all and nothing at the same time. I knew what he was hiding, having used the same expression many times myself. It came in handy on occasions when I had to say stuff like, "No I didn't take your money." Or, "Yes, I did go to school today." And, "But, we did spend the whole sleep-over in Billy's mom's back yard trailer." I had a good idea why he chose to dress in jeans and a tee shirt that would blend so inconspicuously into the crowd

I knew where this kid was going. I was halfway there myself. It wasn't important what happened to him. Who would know or care? Why did it really matter anyway? As far as I could tell, the only thing this guy gave a damn about was crawling away into a dark place where no one could find him. He wanted to cover his trail. A trail I knew all too well, a trail with my name on every road sign.

Handing him back his gun, I said, "Don't think I'll be needin' it where I'm headed." Suddenly, I felt the urge get away, to run fast and far without looking back. But, I sensed that this kid would somehow always be lingering a few short steps behind. Pushing this troubling fantasy out of my head didn't stop the empty feeling that was creeping over me. There had to be a better life for me out there somewhere.

The teen tucked the revolver under his jacket. He crossed the street towards central San Leandro. After watching him

4

fade into the past, I climbed on the AC Transit bus, took a seat and waited for the driver to turn us around.

It was the end of the line. After a few minutes, we began our journey towards San Francisco. Approaching downtown Oakland, all of the white people gradually left the bus. The neighborhood deteriorated. Looking at the iron bars on shop windows and the litter covered sidewalks, thoughts of buying the gun passed fleetingly through my mind. I began to look forward to crossing the Bay Bridge and arriving at the San Francisco bus terminal.

Barely graduating from Ramona High School, I drove my parents to the limits of their patience. By the end of my senior year, dad adopted a "let him go" attitude toward me. After being unable to convince me that my best shot in life would be to become an auto mechanic, he pretty much threw in the towel.

My behavior led both my parents to believe that, I wasn't college material and the time had come for me to get out on my own. Dad must have spoken with his sister because that summer my aunt offered to take me in. I could help out working part time at her A & W Root Beer Stand on MacArthur Blvd. in Oakland. She lived in San Leandro, over 400 miles from Riverside, far enough away to create a major change of environment. They hoped it would somehow ground my unsettled nature. Moving in with my relatives just south of Oakland, I began making regular trips to the city across the bay on my days off.

At eighteen, with no thought of going to college and no particular career goals in mind, I chugged away at menial tasks in my aunt's restaurant. Imagination and constant daydreaming filled the void. Each trip into San Francisco's chilly air sent shivers of life through my body. I roamed the windy streets surrounded by tall glass and steel as crowds of men dressed in suits and women looking spotlessly rich hurried by. I wondered along docks where rough skinned men tended boats tied to piers as seals

5

squealed in the harbor. Soon, the city became a living bustle of wonder. By late September, my mind was filled with dreams of exotic people and mysterious places.

This was, after all, San Francisco in 1963, a city with a long history of rebellious free spirits, a city on the verge of blossoming into the heartland of the flower children. It was a time just before the passing of the mantle. The Beatniks still dominated the North Beach neighborhood. City Lights bookstore filled daily with young men in corduroy and turtle necks. They sported pointy beards and pointy shoes; some even wore French berets. I walked past hipster women in high leather boots, long wool scarves flung over their shoulders. Cool city breezes rolled between the stone and concrete buildings.

The persistently overcast weather spurred my romantic notions about these intriguing folk who appeared so worldly yet, so subdued in their manner. Though understated and downbeat in appearance, I was sure they shared some unspoken secret. As they gathered at the wooden tables of sidewalk cafes, sat on stoops or in back alleyways, a cryptic wisdom emanated from among them. I wanted to be like them, to know what they knew.

Almost always, my starting point for the day's walk was the cable car stop at Powell near the top of Broadway. As I headed down the hill staring out toward the piers along the Embarcadero, a view of the Bay Bridge above and the ocean waters below inspired reverence. A wondrous melancholy overwhelmed my thoughts. It seemed to me that the key to discovering that unspoken Beatnik secret was to roam the world. To succeed, this had to be done in a humble manner. There could be no luxury, no ostentatious behavior. It had to be a journey like that of the Buddha I had learned about in my Unitarian Sunday school, one of observation and labor. It would be a quest for knowledge. I, too, wanted to sit in an alleyway one day and glow with wisdom in the cool foggy shadows.

I began to search in the commercial district for that ship sailing into the great unknown. Most of my visits to the offices of US freighter lines yielded the same comment, "Go talk to the people at the Seaman's Union Hall." This I finally did, only to have my first experience with the insidious union system. The union had set up a double bind. In order to get a job on a freighter, I had to be in the union. In order to get into the union, I had to have a job on a ship. It came down to who I knew, not what I knew or could do. I didn't know anybody.

The Seaman's Union Hall in San Francisco became a perfect spot to feed my imagination. It was an old brick building not far from the International Trade Terminal with oak floors, oak walls, and brass railings. The interior windows, which served as union employees' counters, were enclosed behind black iron bars. Union paperwork passed through a narrow slot at the bottom of these bars. Those teller cages evoked scenes of frontier banks in Wild West movies. Pictures of cargo ships framed in black lacquer and glass hung on the walls. Official looking documents with penned signatures, embossed seals and gold leaf borders judiciously placed around the hall added to the atmosphere of sanctity.

Men with weathered faces clothed in coveralls or jeans and flannel shirts stood around waiting. I had entered a mystical gate keeping temple for the comings and goings of merchant marines moving around the globe. Those images of mighty seafaring vessels chugging bravely over choppy waves hung as silent reminders of great adventure. So many journeys of so many souls still suspended in the ether. Ghosts from the deep blue roamed my thoughts. There were no chairs or benches to sit on. Nothing was designed for permanence.

The staffs' comments discouraging any hope of joining the union faded against the hypnotic backdrop of the building's maritime history. It made me all the more determined to find my ship.

Success up to this point had been illusive. Three weeks of pounding the pavement, left me pretty much where I had started. I needed a new strategy. One of my mothers's many country wisdoms came to mind. *Go straight to the horse's mouth!* kept popping up, interrupting my thoughts. Changing direction, my frontline moved from offices and commercial districts to wooden piers and the waterfront.

Instantly, the world came alive. There was lots of activity along the Embarcadero. Kids and old men fished off the docks. The odor of salt water and dead fish drifted in the breeze. I passed the dark doorways of narrow bars and isolated wooden buildings between the piers. From the corner of my eye, I spotted shadowy figures inside, silhouetted against neon beer signs in mid-morning. Remnants of the night before lingered on; telltale odors of beer and cigarette butts hung in the air. The forlorn sound of Ray Charles played on jukeboxes. I took to whistling the refrain of "Stranger on the Shore" while moving from pier to pier to check out the action.

I was searching for piers with cargo ships and lots of activity. There were no limits on access to freighters. Anybody could walk onto the docks as ships were being unloaded. I climbed gang-planks and roamed decks. Arriving at one busy pier, I watched pallets of wooden cases being lowered ashore. A longshoreman cracked open a case just as one pallet settled on the dock. He pulled a couple of bottles of Dutch beer out of the case. With a mischievous smile, he handed me a bottle. We stood in the shadow of the ship's huge hull, the sea rocking gently below. It was exhilarating to be drinking a rich brew out at the end of the pier. As I stood next to this monstrous structure, tall enough to block all sunlight and a good chunk of the sky, I felt confident that good fortune was now with me.

After talking to some of the seamen, I learned that German and Scandinavian ships took on help, exchanging work for passage to their destinations. They also told me where some of these foreign freighters were docked. Within a

8

week, I had located a captain who wanted to bring aboard some help. He sent me to the offices on the pier. There I filled out some paperwork. I was about to launch into new beginnings aboard the *Cap Finisterre*. In a few days I would be bound for Australia.

Rough Beginnings

The *Cap Finisterre*, a ten thousand ton cargo freighter, had left Hamburg, Germany some five months earlier. She was a great white block of floating metal. Four hatches covering the main cargo hulls stretched the length of the ship. Two smaller decks stood above the main deck. The dining hall, kitchen, and Master Cook's quarters were located on the second deck. A handful of passengers resided on the top deck alongside the captain's quarters. This intimidating steel monolith from a far away land towered above me that morning.

Climbing up the steep gangway, my legs grew heavy, fighting an irreversible pull towards a daunting new fate. My legs had behaved like this once before when, as a ten year old boy, I had climbed down a gloomy set of stairs leading to our coal cellar in Rochester, New York. That night, my folks had left me alone at night for the first time. That was the night that I forced myself to overcome my fear of the dark. I stayed in our bleak basement huddled in a damp corner until being there didn't bother me anymore. Trudging up the metal steps of the gang plank on this foggy San Francisco morning, I felt myself passing beyond another point of no return.

Once on board, the First Mate directed me to the cook's quarters and assigned me the upper of two bunks. The bunk looked tiny. Fortunately my small suitcase fit nicely in the narrow locker provided. I wondered why the cook had chosen the lower bunk, because upper one struck me as more desirable. My job would be to assist the cook in cleaning and waiting tables in the dining hall.

The first day was spent polishing silver, folding linen napkins, and generally getting the dining hall sparkling clean. As I rubbed and scrubbed away at this elegant hall imagining how my subservient role would play out, the captain passed by from time to time. He looked so proper, so austere. I began to wonder about the Captain's motives in taking me aboard. Surely, he was old enough to have known defeat by the Allies some eighteen years earlier. Was his plan to savor the pleasure of being served by the hands of those who had dished up defeat not so very long ago? My thoughts wondered into fantasy as I concocted a scenario akin to something from one of the many World War II films I had watched on TV.

We rocked gently in San Francisco Bay that first day. Having never been at sea, I anxiously anticipated our great voyage with no inkling of the effect rolling waves were about to have on me. My fate would soon change and remain altered for the balance of the voyage.

After completing my chores for the day, I went down to the main deck to explore the ship. The deckhands welcomed my arrival. They seemed as curious about me as I was about them. These guys were very different from the Master Cook who hardly spoke to me, except for his few terse instructions. The Master Cook did not venture off that second deck while the deckhands let me know that they were not allowed on the two upper decks. There appeared to be two worlds on board. The Master Cook and I were balancing between these worlds.

The deckhands struck me as likeable partly because they had an endless supply of beer and shared generously. With plenty of good beer to drink, we exchanged observations about America and Germany in broken English accompanied by lots of gesturing. Unaccustomed to this unpasteurized German beer, or so much free beer, I drank bountifully and it tasted mighty good. The evening passed festively, me struggling to repeat a few words of German accompanied by outbursts of laughter, while guzzling as much beer as I could get into my belly. At least, that is what I think happened before I stumbled off to my cabin and a deep sleep, oblivious to the world as we sailed into the Pacific.

I was abruptly aroused at first light by a ruckus and some loud grumblings in German. As I struggled to achieve consciousness, I became aware of a warm moistness in the bunk. Then it hit me, oh no! Not only had I peed in the bed, I had peed volumes. Even worse, the yellow stream ran along the lower edges of my bunk creating a light drizzle onto the bunk below.

Insisting on the lower bunk had proven an ill-fated decision for the Master Cook. It must have been a rude awakening for this fastidious fellow. He was out of bed in a flash and in a fury. He disappeared yelling. Suddenly a small crowd of witnesses arrived to confirm my foul deed. I was quickly condemned, ordered to pack my belongings, and banished from the second deck forever.

The only good thing about the event was that we were already at sea and out of sight of land. The Captain must have wished we were still close enough to land that he could put me ashore. The next best thing was to exile me from ship society and hope I would fall overboard. My new digs became a seldom used storage locker half way between mid-ship and the bow. A few of the crew dragged a stack of chains and barrels from the locker. A makeshift bed was set up by throwing an old bunk mattress on the steel floor. The other deckhands resided a good distance away at the stern of the ship. With my quarantine completed, this iron vault became home for the next six weeks.

At first, I felt like the Hunchback of Notre Dame without the rock throwing. No one wanted to have anything to do with me. My new job sent me hanging over the side of the ship on some shaky scaffolding to paint the hull white. The sea held fairly calm at first, which must have disappointed the Captain. Shortly, another sailor was stuck doing this job with me. I never found out what he did to deserve it.

From this low point, life gradually began to improve. My new partner, Klaus, and I got to talking in broken English in a friendly way. After all, who else could he count on to yell, "*Mann über Bord*" (man overboard)?" We gained a certain reputation for courage when the other deckhands saw us hanging over the edge, waves lapping at our behinds.

Then, the sea got a bit rougher. Perhaps the Captain reconsidered the prospect of seeing us drown, or just figured we had paid our dues. To our great relief, we were moved back onboard giving us the task of painting the ship's deck and railings grey. Starting at the bow, this job would take a while. Meals were now eaten aft with the rest of the deckhands who gradually decided that I was a decent enough fellow after all. I had earned my sea legs becoming an accepted member of the working class.

To my delight, not only were there three great meals a day, but two additional very hardy snacks. I quickly came to love all those German sausages and that wonderful German beer in all its varieties: although I limited drinking to a bottle or two with the evening meal for the rest of the trip. Some of the meals were very foreign to me. I never could teach myself to like one dish, in particular, which consisted of raw hamburger, chopped onions, and a raw egg. You cracked the egg over the beef and onions mixing it all together. It became a light brownish hash that, after a good stir, looked almost cooked. But it still tasted like uncooked meat and raw eggs. The Galley Cook, not to be confused with my former victim, the Master Cook, was kind enough to save me some sausage and cheese the days they served that dish.

Looking out over the bow, I saw nothing but flat horizon in every direction. It felt like looking into eternity with no end and no beginning, just space and movement. The sunsets grew into a spectacular golden red as that big orange ball sank over the edge of the ocean, pulling its glowing blanket of fire down behind it. The boat rocked steadily forward as the moon took over. Waves crashed against the bow's point, throwing off foaming white whiskers that glowed in the florescence of the moonlight, then faded into blue blackness.

This space, a moment of anticipation suspended in time, took on a purifying quality as we continued to move toward a distant shore. Old feelings dissolved in the salty breezes. A new confidence began to grow under the protection of the Pacific's warm nights. I could bask in wonder at the edge of the universe and then crawl back into my steel cocoon for a night's metamorphosis.

Something happens after long periods of time spent at sea. I was completely removed from the people I knew and the life I lived each day, no longer subjected to my reflection in society's critical eye. On this journey, we had no television, no radio, no newspapers and no mail. There were no movies. The ship was big enough to allow each person some degree of privacy. The daily job was simple and repetitive. People spoke only if they felt like it.

Very slowly, impalpably, a change was taking place. Such a quiet and subtle thing that it became impossible to say exactly what happened. But I changed. I changed forever and the person I was when I stepped on board was no longer the one who stepped off. This new person thought slightly differently, was more circumspect, less defensive. My essence remained intact, my problems traveled with me. It's just that something about me had undergone an emotional shift. My concerns became smaller and less important. A delicate cleansing occurred, a reaffirming of the fragile nature of our relationship with the vastness of the universe. For me, gazing over the bow those many nights, dreaming, shedding that thin layer of skin between me and the world became a vital part of growing up.

Being out of touch with the world long enough, I began to forget things. It was nice not to have the complicated social interactions every day. Still, it was unsettling to forget what the ground felt like under my feet. There really is such a thing as sea legs. But, most incredible for a young man, I began to forget what it felt like to have girls around.

There were only men on this ship. As time passed, a lot of sexual energy got stored up and tension mounted. The crew started to talk about women more frequently. Some of the men had pin-up style photos over their bunks or an image torn from a magazine. To my surprise, it became more and more difficult to remember key details like the sound of a female voice or the smell of their hair. Women became two-dimensional like the pictures in the magazines. When we learned we were a day out from Pago Pago in the Samoan Islands and planned to dock there overnight, that evening the mess hall hummed with anticipation like a Christmas Eve gala, even Santa would have jumped for joy.

Samoa, a Mysterious Island

The sight of land was a thrilling event after weeks of rolling on the waves surrounded by endless ocean. The more seasoned sailors were the first to spot the island. It appeared, at first, only a speck on the horizon. Then word spread quickly where to search for it. Our entertainment for the better part of the morning was watching that speck grow into a grey mound, until finally it became a mountain of lush green tropical foliage interspersed with tall palm trees. Pago Pago sat back in the apex of a funnel shaped bay. Passing through the bay, we followed a route a few hundred yards offshore while an exotic scene gradually unraveled before us.

A coastline of gentle rolling hills came into view. In the clearings atop the knolls were huts consisting of four wooden poles supporting thickly thatched roofs. The huts

14

had raised wood floors encircled by bamboo railings with brightly colored cloths hanging over them. Galvanized metal buckets and other utensils lay strewn around the clearings in front of the huts. These apparent living quarters had no windows and no doors. Amber skinned people, loosely or partially clad in multicolored fabrics, stopped to take a look at our passing ship. They seemed unmoved, as if our presence was nothing out of the ordinary.

For me, however, these were magical creatures, living in an enchanted paradise. The sun shone bright and warm that day. The occasional light rain that fell on us did not even seem like rain. It evoked that refreshing feeling of running through a sprinkler in the summer sun. Finally, we arrived at the only pier in port, a graying wooden structure paralleling the shore. We tied up alongside it.

The port of Pago Pago was a small and quiet place. A handful of two story buildings peppered the hillside connected by a network of dirt roads that fanned out from the concrete and corrugated metal warehouse next to the dock. These were old colonial style buildings designed for functionality: white wooden boxes with gray roofs set against rich tropical greens. We spent the rest of the day onboard pretending to work while taking in this island panorama. Calm settled over the ship as we waited, anxious to feel the earth beneath our feet.

I followed the older seamen who knew where sailors were welcome. They led me to a bar in one of these colonial structures. Inside, a few island beauties in brightly colored outfits served us drinks and took our money. We all began to decompress with beer and wine as catalysts. The firewater poured into our bellies only kindled the fire in our loins. Our hostesses became Goddesses commanding the attention of all eyes.

The few locals in the bar seemed to be enjoying the bawdy joking around. One short stout islander wearing a plaid shirt and plaid khaki shorts came over to our table. Pulling up the chair next to me, he asked. "How long you guys been at sea?"

"Three weeks. Ground beneath my feet feels great!" I replied, continuing to stare at the island girls.

"Got some hot mamas here, ay. Let me buy you boys a round of beers."

At that, Klaus turned and extended his hand. "I'm Klaus. A beer sounds damned good. You from round here?"

"Oh, yah, got lot a business on the island." At this comment, Klaus turned back to watching the hostesses wiggle by as they circulated between tables and the bar.

"What kind of business is there here? When we came in this morning, I didn't see much business, nothin' but a few wooden buildings." I said.

"Behind the palms, can't see much from a ship. Dirt roads hook up the island towns. Never been here before?" The islander searched my face.

"Nope, first time at sea"

"Must be lonely for you. Miss the family, do you?"

"Hell no, this is great! Here's to a sailor's life." I tapped my beer bottle against his and guzzled down a big swig while turning to the girls. One of the Goddesses stepped up to a microphone. An alluring tropical melody began to flow from her thick lips as she swayed side to side.

It didn't take long to finish that beer. Moments later, our new friend drew my attention away from the girls again as he put his hand on my shoulder. "Have another beer on me; let's drink to the sailor's life, as you say. My name is George by the way." He stuck out his thick hand.

I shook his hand, "Nice to meet you George. George what?"

"Just George."

"Well, thanks for the beer, George. I'm Richard." I turned again to the singing girl whose dress was wrapped tightly around her waist with a long slit up one side. Her beautiful brown skin provided an exotic contrast with her flowery white dress. I detected two exciting mounds firmly held beneath it.

After a few more beers generously provided by George, I started to feel pretty good. I leaned back, watching the German sailors who tossed out flattering comments to the girls in broken English with increasing frequency. They joked wantonly with the waitresses, handing the pretty ladies generous tips. The girls teased back with flirtatious smiles.

Just as things were heating up, George turned to face me. "Got to go collect the box office money from my cinemas. Want to come with me, see the island? I have a case of beer in the jeep. Drink some beers on the way."

It seemed like something wild was about to break loose in the bar. I didn't want to leave the beauties. Still, I had never seen any place like this island and was curious to explore. We would be heading out to sea in the morning. Besides, I had no money with me and George had a case of beer. I decided to go.

Outside, George started the engine of his olive green army jeep. It had no top. A case of beer balanced invitingly on the back seat. I climbed into the passenger's side, grabbed a beer and popped open the bottle as we rolled down a narrow road between the palms.

We arrived at the first cinema which surprised me by being so different from those back home. There was no real building. It was hardly a theater at all, a screen suspended between two poles in the middle of a clearing. A few rows of long wooden benches had been lined up in front of the canvas display. Behind them, a small wooden shack served as a ticket booth and concession stand. Periodically some of the few dozen spectators present shouted excitedly at the screen.

While George collected money pouches from an islander behind the door of the wooden shack, I sat down in the back on one of the long benches. Afterwards, George came over and sat very close to me on the log bench.

"So how you like my island? Warm here isn't it. No need to wear much clothing."

"It's a cool place, well, warm I mean, but why are they yelling at the screen?" I slid over just a bit.

"Oh, they think. The people on the screen are real. They try to talk to them. Come on, we have more theaters to take care of." He handed me another beer.

Several theaters later, after a lot of driving, too much beer, and far more time than I wanted to spend away from the Goddesses, I began to tire of meandering through the countryside even though the island was beautiful. "Let's go back, man, its gettin' late and I wanta see what's happenin' at the bar."

"Just one last stop, the best stop of all. I'm taking you to the most beautiful view on the island, lovely spot."

The jeep pulled up a hill that overlooked the Pacific. The pale light that filled the horizon radiated from an almost full moon in a clear sky. A bamboo and straw hut stood silhouetted against an expanse of blue. As we rolled to a stop, George's voice changed. He began to speak, softly, almost in a whisper.

"This is my favorite spot. The view from that hut over there's breath taking. Let's go over there. I'll lie on the mat; you could do me hard from behind. Work off all that load of energy in me. Take as long as you like."

As he spoke, George slid his hand up my left thigh slowly approaching my crotch. That got my attention, quickly sobering me up. I felt very uncomfortable. Before George's hand had traveled too far, I grabbed his wrist and removed his hand. In as firm a tone as I could muster, I said, "You've picked the wrong guy for that stuff. Don't wana do that? Just take me back to the bar!"

To my amazement, this was all it took to change his behavior. George gripped the steering wheel with both hands looking sullen, as we headed back to port. We did not talk on the way back. He refused to drive to the bar, but rather dropped me off at the ship, waiting until I was up the ramp before he left.

This crazy island safari with George had used up a lot of valuable time. Maybe I had missed out on all the fun back at the bar. As soon as George left, I scrambled down the ramp two steps at a time and rushed off towards the bar.

At two in the morning, the bar was deserted except for the bartender who was cleaning up. When I asked him where everyone had gone, he pointed to a small doorway, suggesting that what I sought was down there. I descended a few wooden steps into a crawl space tucked below the bar. It was no more than four feet high with straw mats scattered over the dirt floor.

Sure enough, there lay three of my shipmates scattered around the floor sleeping. At their epicenter, one of the Goddesses lay curled up in a fetal position. Her lovely brown thighs protruded casually beyond her hiked up skirt. I had missed the party. Unsure how these situations might be handled, I decided to take a bold action. Borrowing George's technique from earlier that evening, I gently slid my hand under her skirt and up her thigh, stopping when I felt pubic hair against the edge of my hand. That woke her up.

The outcome, however, was not what I had hoped. Only half awake, she tossed around a bit pushing my hand aside. She mumbled "no no no sore tired."

Waving her hand vaguely around, she seemed to be implicating those sleeping males that encircled her. She uncer-

19

emoniously rolled over and went back to sleep. This is how my first experience with the adult world of sex began and abruptly ended.

Arriving in the land of Upside Down

The next day, we sailed, somewhat uneventfully, away from this tropical paradise. Looking back from time to time, the rich greens slowly faded to gray. Finally, the island became a shrinking speck that vanished beyond the horizon. It began to feel as if that place and those exotic people had never really existed.

The next two weeks went by quickly as we resumed our routine life. We had crossed well beyond the halfway point of our journey. Everyone felt comfortable with each other. Everything settled back into place as we returned to our routines. My quarters had become a private retreat. It turned out to be a kind of bonus since all the other deckhands slept two to a cabin.

For this last leg of the trip, the ocean was calm, the air warm and clean. I felt a great sense of freedom. It seemed strange to feel so liberated and yet be confined to a few hundred yards of walking space and eight feet of sleeping space. The unique mix of time and distance further facilitated my break with the past. Another shell of social constraint peeled away. The old rules that influenced me back home no longer applied. Wilder currents of desire, curiosity, and rebellion, already present in me, rose closer to the surface. Out of this laissez-faire world of rugged sailors arose a new set of guidelines for my moral standards. I was ready to rage against the wind, consequences be damned.

Focus shifted to our arrival in the port of Sydney. Through talks with the sailors, Australia began to take shape as a real place. They described a land where jobs were plentiful, where working permits could be easily obtained. Luck seemed to be traveling at my side, as I had only twenty dollars left and would need a job very soon. The sailors even knew where to go to get all the immigration papers in order.

It was mid-October which, surprisingly, was also good news. We had arrived in the land of upside down where summer was winter and, best of all, winter was summer. A long stretch of good weather awaited us. A particularly fortunate circumstance since sleeping on the beach, which had become a distinct possibility, now sounded like a reasonably pleasant one. According to my wise German friends, the Australian women were all friendly and beautiful. No one worked too hard, and the beer was *almost*, as good as the German brands I had grown so fond of over the past month and a half.

Nearing in the port of Sydney started out like the spotting of Pago Pago, a growing speck on the horizon. But this speck grew into a monolith of endless shoreline. As we approached land, our ship was gradually overwhelmed. Not only were there many other bigger cargo ships flying the flags of many nations, but there were tall luxurious looking cruise ships, sailboats, ferryboats, tugboats, and a gargantuan bridge. We became a small float in a massive pageant.

Towering buildings erased any thought of palm trees. Two tugboats harnessed our ship and towed us to one of the many piers that jetted out in all directions. Several tall cranes hovered over our decks, thick steel claws readied to remove our four protective hatches. We were back in the grips of western civilization.

A stretch of beautiful coastline could be seen off to the north, rolling green hills with cozy wooded knolls and red brick houses tucked away among the trees. The sun was shining as a new kind of excitement filled the air, the promise of a fresh start. In this land, anything would be possible. New people were taking us into their world. People that spoke English with a funny twang. These long-shoremen seemed relaxed, joking and laughing as they secured our ship to their shores. These easy going, happy people welcomed us whole-heartedly on that bright morning.

Sure enough, the Germans knew what they were talking about. Both Customs and Immigration offices could be found near the docks. They seemed ready, even eager, to stamp my passport with a working visa. No one asked any questions about my financial status. Agents quickly directed me to the offices across the way. Clerks in the Employment Agency offered me a job on the spot working in a factory. Never had it been so easy to get a job. I went back to the *Cap Finisterre* to celebrate the good news with my shipmates.

Of course, the Germans knew about a bar near our ship. We eagerly awaited evening to celebrate with some drinking and general carousing. This bar, in the heart of Sydney's docks, was quite different from the one in the tropics. It was big. The large rectangular hall surrounded us in brass and hardwood. The pub's countertop, floors, and walls were constructed from oak. Stepping up to the bar, there were brass footrests below with brass guard rails above.

Two or three bartenders corralled inside the oval oak counter served patrons wrapped two deep around it. People were drinking a lot and very jubilant. Scattered here and there, beautiful feminine creatures wiggled about in scant outfits. This time, I got it: they were not exactly women. If we were willing to believe their illusion, they would probably provide some form of sexual satisfaction. Most of our crew came for laughs and booze. Some of the guys had already left in search of more serious activity at the nearby brothels. A small group of sexy things next to us flirtatiously asked the bartender to show me and Klaus his "invention". It was a thick wooden ruler with a sliding marker. They used it to measure the length of your "instrument". Yes, some of these girlish creatures were very enticing. It was, nevertheless, time for me to move on from this kind of experience.

My ship-painting buddy told me about the local night life spot, a place called "King's Cross". We only needed to climb the hill a ways, well within walking distance from the docks. My fellow painter and I declined to be measured. The two of us left the pub and headed up the hill toward what we hoped would be more fertile stomping grounds.

King's Cross spread out from a major intersection lit up by lots of bright neon signs whose glow guided us from afar. People milled about in an area a few blocks wide. We picked a corner bar and went in for a few beers. Inside the smoke-filled hall, couches and chairs clustered about the bar. A jukebox played softly in the background. There were mostly men inside. The few real women present sat in groups accompanied by men. The atmosphere appeared more informal, than exciting, with lots of casual conversation.

We ordered a couple beers and got to talking, as we usually did, in broken English using simple words. Some of the men around us heard my American accent and my friend's German accent. They joined in with questions about us, and our respective countries.

One member of our newly formed group, a young man close to my own age, introduced himself as Dwayne. He claimed to be half American and half Australian. His red hair and freckles gave him the air of those Irish kids I had known in Upper State New York.

I eventually got around to describing my predicament of being newly employed, but a bit strapped for funds and not quite sure where to go next. Luck was still at my side. Dwayne told me he lived with his recently divorced mother in a flat near Bondi Beach. They were looking for renters to occupy the front room as they needed extra income. He offered to rent me the room with no payment due until after my first payday. On a handshake, we agreed to the terms. Dwayne gave me directions as we arranged to meet at the flat the next morning.

That night I ran up against an unfamiliar Australian policy. All the hotels that sold alcohol were obliged by law to close their doors at ten p.m. It was a sort of a modified prohibition to get men home at a decent hour. If they went home sober, that was an added bonus. We returned to the *Cap Finisterre* a bit on the early side for a good night's sleep.

The next day, grabbing my suitcase and bidding farewell to this great bunch of German sailors, I returned to land-lover status. It was a simple ending to what had proven to be a great adventure. It was also a simple beginning to great new one.

The Land Down Under
CHAPTER TWO

Settling In

It was a warm Sunday morning. The tram rolled along Bondi Road, heading south out of the center of Sydney. The city gradually gave way to neighborhoods as dense structures grew scarce, replaced by rows of two story buildings; often with flats over the street level businesses. Families strolled about window shopping at closed stores or lingered in front of restaurants. Eighty-three Spring Street was located only a few short blocks south of Bondi Junction on a quiet street. The flat sat on the second story of a modest two unit building. Dwayne greeted me at the door with his mother by his side. He was taller than I remembered; almost my height of 6'4, yet his mother stood only a bit over five feet. Mary had a strong, coarse voice. She spoke clearly, sparingly and always with conviction. She explained house rules to me, leaving no room for doubt that everyone would abide by them

"Your personal belongings go in your closet. Don't leave them about the flat. Keep the kitchen and bathroom clean at all times; no girls allowed to sleep over; and, no noise on weeknights after 10 pm." she declared. The rules were simple and fair.

Mary struck me as a reasonably attractive woman with sparkling eyes and red hair. Her body was toned and muscular, yet quite feminine. She sounded Australian and looked Irish. In spite of her toughness, she exuded a kind of warmth that inspired confidence. I knew living here was going to be easy.

It took only two minutes to see the entire flat. Mary lived in the back room, across from the kitchen. Dwayne had his own room next to Mary's. A small living room with a window offering a view of the flat next door divided the apartment. My room was at the front of the flat. Its window overlooked the street. A long hallway connected all the rooms.

The three small beds crammed into the front room left barely enough space to stand between them. Three small armoires lined up against one wall. To my surprise, two other people would share the room with me. No wonder the rent was so low. Dwayne had rounded up a couple of Canadian immigrants from King's Cross much as he had done with me. The Canadians showed up later that morning in high spirits. I settled in, unpacking my clothes into one of the armoires. Everyone got along fine, in spite of the cramped quarters.

Monday morning, I hopped a bus eager to start my new job at Dunn Carpet Products. I had no idea what "under felt" was, much less how it was made, I had never worked in a factory or even visited one.

The Dunn factory looked pretty dull, surrounded by warehouses. The place, shaped like a giant rectangular box, had no windows. A sign bolted over the entrance read "Dunn's Carpet Products" in square red lettering. I entered into an office area where a half dozen metal desks spread out across the carpet. Rows of grey filing cabinets lined up against one wall beyond which a handful of cubicles created from clusters metal partitions with glass tops served as offices. The dozen or so people that worked here wore dull sports coats and ties or frumpy dresses.

The foreman, Tony, introduced himself and offered to show me around. From the entrance to the main factory, I could see scattered groups of crude machinery bolted to the concrete floor. These machines were driven by large electric motors painted in olive greens and flat grays. They formed numbered workstations. Tony handed me a mask to cover my mouth and nose. Elastic straps wrapped behind my head holding a molded rubber shell with its cloth breathing filter against my face.

As soon as we entered the shop floor, things got nasty. Visibility shrunk to only a few feet, as a cloud of dark particles filled the air. Large clumps of grey/brown fibers the

27

size of baked beans floated from the floor to chest level while smaller particles rose to seven or eight feet off the ground. These specks hung like dark stars silhouetted against the yellow glow from rows of long cylindrical bulbs suspended on chains high overhead. Pounding noises rattled the air.

"Under felt" turned out to be the material used under carpets. It served as a buffering layer between the sub-floor and the carpet. At Dunn's, these were made out of old burlap bags or other scrap fabrics, generally coarse and deteriorating. Dunn's received truckloads of the stuff.

The first job Tony offered me was that of operator of one of the "decompressing" stations. Burlap bags stacked four feet high waited on wooden pallets facing an iron-jawed crusher. The operator fed burlap by hand into a six inch opening between two metal plates five foot square. Both upper and lower plates were densely packed with four inch nail-like teeth. The heavy steel jaws pulled apart, and then slammed together again with a loud thud. This job would require me to feed burlap bags between those jaws which pulverized them into shredded clouds of fiber. This puffy conglomeration formed a swirling tail as it disappeared out the other side of the jaws. The dense flow was drawn out and captured by a roaring suction pump attached in the back of the machine. The pulp eventually settled into large carts on wheels parked behind the pump.
Tony jokingly advised that I would have to stay alert if I chose this job. The current operator held up a calloused hand with two fingers missing. He grinned and they both had a good laugh. The humor escaped me. His three-fingered hand was more than I needed to see!

We progressed through the gloomy particle fog, from workstation to workstation, through the back door and out onto a loading dock. The air cleared, and the noise dropped off. Tall rolls of under felt lay stacked against the wall as a worker loaded them onto trucks. A job opening existed here to help load the trucks. Without hesitation, I volunteered for it.

At first, throwing around fifty pound rolls of under felt left me pretty sore by evening. After a few weeks I got used to it. My co-workers were a friendly bunch and we often lunched together at a nearby pub or at one of the small neighboring sandwich shops. I began to learn Australian ways and lingo. I quickly caught on that men were called "blokes" and women "sheilas". Daily greetings went something like "Goodai, aharye mate?" followed by "Arrite, I reckon". Many afternoons wound down with "guddanye mate, howsabout us mob knock down a cupla skooners". Then off to the pub we went with beers all round.

Fridays were paydays. It was pretty much the same every week. Pick up the pay check after work, go directly to the bank, and convert it to cash. Then, with pockets full of money, head straight to the pubs. I fudged a bit, systematically putting ten percent of my weekly income into a savings account before spending most of the rest over the weekend like everyone else.

If there were four of us going out after work, no one left the pub before the first four beers. Australian etiquette required that whoever bought the first round of beers would, in turn, receive a free beer on the next round. It was mandatory for everyone to buy a round of beers before any discussion of leaving for the next pub would be tolerated.

The drinking age of eighteen in Australia made me legal. No one seemed to care. Not once did I spot a bartender asking to see I.D.s. Freedom to drink oneself silly appeared to be a sacred cultural mandate. Not only my co-workers, but all of my roommates as well, headed off to get loaded as soon as they had cashed their paychecks. The King's Cross district became our haunt of preference. Many a weekend passed in a never ending flow of beer, barroom philosophizing, and joking around. My mentorship had passed from German sailors to the Australian working man.

Drinking got out of control at times. One particular Saturday morning in mid summer, I sat on my small bed writing a second entry in my newly acquired journal while sipping from a coffee cup half filled with whisky. I felt lousy. My mates assured me a shot of hard liquor the next day was the best thing to do to avoid a bad hangover. The night before, I had narrowly escaped death lurking at the bottom of a whisky bottle.

Dwayne and I got into one-upmanship bantering after a night of pints at the pub. Dwayne challenged me to a drinking contest. We each bought a fifth of Johnny Walker and faced off. Sitting in the front room on two small beds with a nightstand between us, we poured shot after shot of whisky down our throats. Then we compared bottles to see who had the most left. This went on until I blacked out. My roommates told me the next morning that I had dropped, back first, onto the bed. I was choking on my own vomit when they found me. They dragged me out back and I filled a mop bucket with vomit before they washed me down with a hose. They got me to drink some water and put me to bed. That Saturday morning I sat on the couch drinking water, trying to recover quickly so as not to miss out on the upcoming evenings' pub crawl.

Kangaroo Boxing

Shortly after settling into my new home in Bondi Junction, I discovered beautiful Bondi beach. Surfing Newport Beach in the summers of my high school years had been a lot of fun, but Bondi put that beach to shame. The brisk mile walk from our flat to the ocean was pleasant on a warm day. The tram also took passengers directly there from a stop at Bondi Junction just down the block from our flat.

30

On a good day at Newport Beach, two to four foot swells rolled in evenly and smoothly. At Bondi, the waves were four to six feet high and rolled in just as nicely. Bondi was a very long beach where the swells formed a good distance off shore allowing for long rides. After my first visit, I knew I had to surf Bondi. Amazingly, there were not many surfers in Australia which left plenty of distance between boards in the bay. I soon purchased a used surfboard frequently spending weekends at Bondi Beach.

The two Canadians sharing our room also quickly adapted to the Australian lifestyle and colorful slang. Between them, they managed to buy a used car. Phil actually owned the car. He was about six feet tall with a wiry body and quick temper. Art was shorter and very muscular, but he had a gentle disposition. We became friends while living in such close quarters. Even though they did not surf, both were fun loving hearty drinkers who often frequented the pubs along the beach. Many a sunny weekend afternoon was spent putting away pints of beer in the many seaside pubs just down the road on Bondi beach.

One warm Saturday morning, we drove down to Bondi beach in their new car. I went to surf while Art and Phil hit the pub for some grub and beer. As he planned on doing some serious drinking, Phil gave me his car keys to drive them back later. I headed down the beach for a little surfing. When I returned to the pub late in the afternoon, Phil and Art were not there. I searched for them at the bar next door to no avail. Figuring they had decided to enjoy the sun and make the short walk home, I drove back to the flat. Though, I felt some hesitation at possibly having left them behind. It was not my car. When I reached the flat, no one was home. It bothered me that they were not there yet. I walked around the neighborhood looking for them in the local watering holes. Thinking they would show up soon, I returned to the flat, got out of my swimming trunks and showered.

This touchy situation exploded half way through my shower. The plastic curtain suddenly flew back revealing a very drunk, very angry Phil staring me in the eye.

"You stole my car, you bloody bastard!" he shouted, red in the face, fists clenched.

Phil threw my swimming trunks at me. "Get this on now! You're goin' out da street for a proper wallopin'!"

I was frightened and confused. This was worse than peeing on the cook's head!

An odd mix of circumstances determined the outcome of what followed. Between surfing and loading trucks, I had gotten my body in great shape. At the same time, I thought violence was wrong and should never be used. The tales of eastern religion they told us in my Unitarian Youth Group mingled with images of Holden Caulfield, the anti-hero of Catcher in the Rye, lead me to believe that real Beatniks practiced pacifism. However, none of the Australians I met shared my admiration of Beatniks or any of my curious notions about pacifism. Few in this rough crowd would have wanted to miss out on enjoying a good fight. My non-violent babblings on the occasional drunken evening out had left Phil, Art, and Dwayne indifferent. What happened next came as a surprise to everyone.

After quickly slipping on my trunks while receiving the occasional shove or slap to the head, I found myself in front of Phil being pushed down the steps to the street.

"This is a misunderstanding. You're my friend. I thought you walked back to the flat," I pleaded to a drunken angry Phil.

My pleas for reason just made him angrier, more aggressive. When we were on the sidewalk, I turned around looking directly into the eyes of someone no longer recognizable. He was lost in a drunken fury, intent on satisfying a sadistic desire for revenge. His eyes glowed with self-confidence at the prospect of gratification. Thrilled by his sense of power over me, Phil flailed away aiming for my head and upper body. Most of his blows landed on my arms or missed completely. Being taller and sober, fending off his attacks came easily at first. More agile, I bought time to apologize and pleaded with him to stop. My groveling fueled his excitement. He attempted to improve the accuracy and power of the shots. It was getting harder to avoid being hit.

"When I've finished, they'll scrape your bloody piker arse off the pavement!" he screamed. I stopped talking. Confronted with such contempt, my pacifism vanished. I faced the prospect of a serious beating. Phil thrived on my passivity. My lack of response lulled him into a complacent unprotected stance, leaving him vulnerable.

I began to look for the right opening while narrowly avoiding blows, which grew harder, if not more precise. The opening came after a wild swing that exposed the left side of his face. Summoning all my strength, I swung at his head. My right fist landed dead center on his left temple. Phil's face went blank, his arms fell to his sides; he crumpled, a boneless blob of flesh, to the pavement. A few minutes passed in silence with no movement.

Finally, looking shaken and disoriented, he rose slowly to a sitting position. I could not believe it. Reconciliation flashed across my mind. For this conflict to end with the restoration of some harmony in the weeks to come, Phil needed a way to save face. I began to apologize and back away, making declarations of regret. When he finally staggered to his feet no rage remained. It was a surprised and subdued person who slowly climbed up the stairs to the flat.

From that day on, an uneasy silence charged with undercurrents of hostility lingered between us. Phil and Art continued to share the front room until early fall when they moved to their own place. Our paths never crossed again. Apparently, Beatniks had no run-ins with the likes of Phil.

My attitude toward pacifism descended from an article of faith to a topic of debate.

After the Canadians moved out, Dwayne had difficulty finding new renters willing to put up with sharing the room. He and I began to hang out together a lot more, becoming closer. Mary felt he needed a friend. She grew more sympathetic behaving in a slightly kinder and more generous way towards me. The three of us ate supper together on occasion. We worked out a new arrangement. Mary only increased my rent slightly and the entire front bedroom became mine for the rest of my stay in Australia.

Dwayne got a new job in late summer. He started training as a male nurse at Callan Park, Sydney's largest mental hospital. Within a month he had arranged an interview for me. The hospital accepted me into the nurses training program. Quitting Dunn's, I took a few weeks to relax with only the occasional one-day construction work for pocket money.

One builder's laborer job led to an unsettling experience. We were to move some earth on a grading job, leveling an area to pour foundation for a new structure at the University of Sydney. It was good physical exercise which I plunged into whole heartedly earning the favor of the foreman. He acknowledged my effort by offering to make me his assistant-trainee.

One day, while I stood in the center of the university covered in dirt, shovel in hand, the courtyard filled with college students. Girls and boys my own age cut across the quad, coming and going to classes. They were clean and well dressed. Some sat around on benches chatting, others walked to class passing just a few feet away. Not one of them noticed me. I would have loved to mingle among so many of my peers, but it was as if I did not exist I was just another mound of dirt, more invisible than the concrete. At that moment, I felt myself a common ditch digger building structures for the enjoyment of my betters. Had my father's disappointment in his son's future been justified? That story about the invisible man sunk in with brutal clarity. Declining the foreman's offer, I took the day's pay to spend it on beer and grub in the pub with my mates.

Callan Park

A week later I sat on the bus headed for Callan Park. What a grandiose landscape appeared before me, the gates growing taller as the bus approached. Situated on Iron Cove, these 100-year-old grounds contained several two-story sandstone buildings surrounding a large courtyard. The stones that formed the walls were quarried from the earth on site. Other buildings were scattered around the grounds, gracefully separated by green lawns and tall shade trees. Elegant iron fencing that meandered down to the sleepy banks of the Parramatta River enclosed the sprawling compound. I began to wonder if its walls were meant to keep patients in or visitors out. Sydney University's stone and concrete campus paled before this majestic tranquility.

Once inside the 61-acre site with the gates locked behind me, I started to get nervous. What did it mean to be mad and what frightening acts were crazy people capable of committing? The staff greeted me warmly and gave a brief orientation of the hospital and my duties. The uniform issued to me included a pair of dark blue/gray trousers with a matching shirt and black belt. The heavy shirt sported two round shoulder patches. The patches had official looking lettering woven across them in thick gold thread. They evoked the demeanor of a prison guard more than that of a nurse. I was relieved to learn that on each ward a mentor would assist me for the first few weeks. Over the next six months, I would be rotated through each of the eleven wards in order to become familiar with the manner in which each was administered. On the job experience would be followed by a period of classroom training.

That first day, the head nurse sent me to one of the calmer wards. Patients dressed in ordinary street clothing wandered about the halls behaving quite normally. No one exhibited the slightest odd behavior. This was an open ward in one of the outer buildings. Its large dormitory slept some thirty patients. The French doors in the main sitting room opened onto a patio, green lawns and an unobstructed view of the river. The openness of the hall evoked the atmosphere of a retreat or spa. Friendly dogs trotted in and out of the dormitory faithfully accompanying the patients. A large dinning hall and kitchen next to the dormitory served quite decent meals on the spacious, well lighted tables. All the meals were prepared and served by the patients.

My duties here required only oversight since the patients diligently did all the necessary chores. A social order clearly prevailed among these "abnormal" people. Observation of the behavior on this ward taught me the "ten to one" rule. Of the thirty or so patients, twenty cleaned up after themselves regularly. It was always the same two or three people who did all the extra work around the dorm, removing the trail of debris and messes left by the same four or five or six patients who never cleaned up after themselves. If this pattern of behavior persisted among the mentally ill, I concluded it must be deeply ingrained in all of society. I decided that a close observation of any social gathering would quickly reveal which few made most of the messes and which few cleaned them up.

Near the end of my first week at Callan Park, I noticed itching. Showering one evening, I discovered three swollen red bands, one around my waist and two around my ankles. Upon closer investigation, the bands were really hundreds of small flea bites that followed the line of the elastic in my underwear and socks. Dwayne laughed at my predicament.

"You'll get used to it. I'll come by your ward tomorrow and show you something." Dwayne grinned.

36

The next day he showed up at the dormitory around mid-morning. "Watch this," he said as he gripped the top sheet of one of the beds that had recently been made. With a swift even stroke, he pulled the covers back separating the top and bottom sheets. A wave of small black dots rushed towards the bottom of the bed quickly disappearing under the covers. A small army of fleas had raced to escape the light.

"They live here too." Dwayne laughed. "They travel between the dogs and the patients. Fleas are everywhere in this place. But not to worry, you will get used to them in a few weeks." Such assurances did not make me especially happy. Yet, after a month of itchy red waist and ankles, the swelling disappeared despite the continued presence of fleas. As an unexpected benefit of working at Callan Park, I developed a partial resistance to flea bites.

The first time I worked a closed ward the devastating impact of mental illness became apparent. These wards had thick iron bars on the windows and tightly controlled access. A guard manned the entrance at a small station just inside the first door. He verified IDs controlling passage through the locked inner door. This facility was built like a medieval fortress. The kitchen, dining hall, recreation room and sleeping quarters formed a rectangle around an open-air stone courtyard. Many of the residents of this community enclosed behind thick walls exhibited behavior that demonstrated just how little we understand the power of the mind.

Entering a closed ward for the first time, all the moaning and loud voices immediately set me on edge. It was reassuring to see there were three other nurses on duty. I soon learned to join with a colleague and move around the ward in a team. On these Level Two wards, the patients were not generally violent, but could exhibit unpredictable behavior suddenly, without provocation. All here required more care and attention due to their elevated degree of debilitation.

The most common sight was patients crisscrossing the courtyard talking to, or shouting at, invisible demons. Every morning, Max, a huge man, stood in one corner of the yard blurting out mournful groans. Over six feet tall, he must have weighted well above 300 pounds with long thick arms. His body was covered in large blue, black and red welts. Max would raise one of his massive arms high in the air; then bring it slamming down on some new part of his body. The thunderous blow echoed across the yard producing a new bruise accompanied by a loud grunt. He continued to do this randomly throughout the day. No one ventured too close to Max.

Walter, on the other hand, was quite popular with the math professors at the University of Sydney. Rumors circulated among the nurses that this scrawny fellow had been the subject of several scholarly papers. I enjoyed sitting with him just to listen, attempting to follow the logic of his convoluted banter. Walter surprised as well as confused the listener with a mixture of words and gestures that wove a three dimensional mystery. His monologues challenged the most attentive as his words hung curiously in mid air.

"From overhead layered folds unraveled, hinged left to right across the angular shoulder. Here". Walter said as he looked over his shoulder, "Binding down into stacked one quarter quadrants following upwards, breakaway logarithms' reach out, split into jagged fractions." Walter would wave an arm haphazardly," Circular plows grinding the squared edges rough off the root, half, quarter lengths, extending arcs through the boulders in a forward geodesic spiral, long away, quadratic, over a jagged summit." He vaguely pointed to the outline of the ward's walls against the sky, "On the far away side, you see void, on the other hand, keep tangent with the close up side." Walter abruptly turned his head, bringing his face close to mine, startling me. This talk could go on for hours with a logical rhythm that faded in and out leaving the listener able to follow for a while, only to get lost in his maze again.

Another patient I quickly learned to keep a close watch over was the catatonic stick figure of a man on this same ward. It was easy to forget about such a silent, almost invisible, creature. I tried extending his arm out to his side just to see if he was faking. In a mind-boggling exhibition of tenacity and strength, he kept his arm extended until an hour later when I came over to lower it. On one occasion, I arrived on duty to find him standing over the urinal in the bathroom, his pants and underwear at his knees. The previous shift nurse must have forgotten about him. He was a living Gumby.

Dwayne pulled duty on the Level Three, the criminally insane ward, within a few months of his hire. His tough guy demeanor and a fiery disposition made Dwayne a good candidate to work there. Growing up half American, half Australian in this homogeneous crowd undoubtedly exposed Dwayne to a lot of harassment and more than his share of fights.

My first visit to that ward was just that "a visit". I really was not prepared to deal with it, having heard the stories of killers that chopped their victims in little pieces. Rapists and child molesters abounded on this ward. One patient was reputed to have dug up his victim's corpse for a second passionate session before burying it for good. The armed guard keyed us into the ward, and we started down the main hall with Dwayne a few feet ahead of me. Suddenly, a patient jumped out of nowhere and got right up in my face. He was saying banalities with a sly smile on his face. Uneasy, I realized that while he was talking to me, looking me in the eye, he stood with one of his feet on top on my foot. Stunned, unable to react, it astonished me that someone would do such an odd thing. What was I to do? Intuition signaled a bad situation; he must be attempting to impose some primal dominance over me which called for an immediate and assertive response. Just then Dwayne yelled out for me to hurry up. I quickly moved away leaving this creepy character in the shadows. There were a lot of very scary men in this locked-down facility. Fortunately for me, the hospital did not allow anyone under the age of twenty-one to work there. I was still eighteen.

The most dangerous ward I actually worked was the temporary holding ward. It was dangerous because of the erratic behavior of patients who had no clear diagnosis. One day, Dwayne got hit in the face by a patient while escorting him down a hallway. Showing no sign of anger, the patient calmly turned around in the hall and attacked Dwayne. I always kept on the alert here. The equivalent of a hospital emergency room, this wing held patients admitted as a result of some acute episode, often involving police or medics. After a short stay with lots of medications, they were returned to the community at large. Perhaps the most unsettling aspect was that several of these patients had familiar faces. They were people we occasionally saw hanging around in the pubs at King's Cross.

A Night of Inside Out

One Friday night a chance meeting took place that caught me "off guard", in more ways than one. My co-worker, Tony, and I had just gotten off duty at Callan Park a bit late that evening. Tony was much like my Canadian friend, Art. He was about five foot nine, muscular, thick boned and burley. In contrast to his tough appearance, he had a gentle nature. Still in our uniforms, we decided to go directly from work to the Victoria Arms, a popular pub on one of the major intersections in King's Cross.

After we chose a spot at the bar, I got things started. "The first round's on me mate." I ordered a couple of KB Lagers on tap and leaned against the bar. "Somethin must a gotten under Max's skin really bad today, mate. He knocked himself silly all morning."

"Had a busy one myself. A new lot showed up at the holding ward this morning. Assignin' digs, handin' out duds.

Checkin' meds. A pint sounds bloody good right about now." Tony sipped his draft.

We continued to talk shop through the first few rounds of beers. Just as my turn to buy rolled around again, this guy a few years older than me come over and joined us. He looked a bit unkempt, but mostly pretty ordinary and of average build.

"You blokes work at Callan Park?" he asked.

"How di'ja know, mate? We just got off work a bit ago," Tony said.

"Recognize that uniform. I've seen a few of those before."

"Worked there too, did you?" Tony asked.

"Not exactly, but I've done my share of business with the place. Know my way around the joint. If a bloke didn't know better, he'd think you were bus drivers."

Tony was quick to pick up on that remark. "Bus drivers might be a step up, mate. I could sit on my arse all day an' sneak grog."

"I'm Craig in case you're dying to know. What you blokes go by."

"Tony and Richard, the hard workin team." I smiled.

"Workin on the inside, hey, I reckon that takes special talents for you blokes. Those uniforms don't tell the whole story. Christ, coppers got uniforms, badges and guns. Supposed to protect a bloke, but that don't mean they ain't got an eye on your every move." Craig seemed like he was getting a bit agitated. Maybe he noticed my brow beginning to furrow because he abruptly switched gears. An all-knowing grin came across his face.

"Here's to you mates, the next shout's on me." Craig beckoned the bar tender while continuing to talk. "What I'm sayin' is; things ain't always as they seem. Can't never be too sure about people. You heard about them two street

41

urchins over in St. James Park the other day?" Craig looked at us smiling quizzically as we stood, blank faced.

"Reckon you didn't. Couple a kids was hanging out in the park when they seen a man wearing a white shirt and a black coat. He was sittin' on one o' them park benches across the path. The first kid asks the other, 'is that the Archbishop of Canterbury over there?' 'Maybe,' the second kid says. So the first kid says, 'Why don't you go ask him?'

"So the second kid goes over, taps the man on the shoulder and asks, 'Are you the Archbishop of Canterbury?' The man looks up from his paper and hollers 'Piss off, kid.' When the kid goes back, his buddy asks, 'Well, was it the Arch Bishop of Canterbury?' 'Donno, he didn't say.'"

We all had a good laugh at Craig's joke which started a whole round of joke telling between beers. After several more rounds and a good deal of joking about conditions at Callan Park, we worked ourselves into a pretty good mood. Unfortunately, the bar's closing bell rang announcing that ten p.m. had rolled around. We would soon be out on the street. Neither Tony nor I felt much like calling it a night.

"What say you blokes come round to my place and down some more grog? I got a few bottles in my room," Craig said. His offer sounded too good to pass up. Tony and I agreed to tag along.

Craig took us to an older neighborhood across town. Our new pal lived in a small studio that faced the street on the ground floor. As we stumbled across the threshold of an old brownstone building, we entered a room with plaster pealing from dirty almond colored walls, cobwebs hung from the corners of the high ceiling. One large bed was pushed up against the far corner of the room. On the street side of the room, a narrow wooden table sat under the sill of a tall window with two chairs placed on either side of the table. Clothes spilled out from the shelves and drawers of a decrepit walnut armoire. The place smelled of dirty

42

laundry. On the back wall of the room, above the bed, a long narrow window overlooked an interior courtyard. The single light bulb screwed into a grey metal shade hung high overhead by a cloth cord. Its dull light dripped down, soaked up by pale walls. This dingy hole put a strain on our previously jovial mood. However, our host did have beer which helped renew our enthusiasm. We were already pretty drunk. I was beginning to feel dizzy.

As Craig wrenched the top off of a Foster's Ale, his mood drew darker. "You damned nurses aren't really nurses, you're bloody jailers. Who you think you're kiddin'? Nobody gives a damn about the people inside." Craig's voice grew more hostile. He slammed the beer on the table. "I been in and out of that place many times. You bludgers pumped me full o' drugs. You think I donno you're tryin' to keep me stupid. You bastards tryin' to control my mind. Want to pin me down, strap me in. You tryin' to kill me, you bloody bastards."

Craig turned red in the face. He stomped over to the armoire, reached into one of the drawers and pulled out a revolver. He began to waive it at me and Tony. Then he pointed the weapon at my head yelling. "I'm gona kill you, both of you, before you can muck me up again. I know what you rotten bastards are thinkin'!"

Tony stepped quickly behind Craig, grabbing him. Tony slid both of his arms behind Craig's neck forcing Craig's body downward, locking him under control. Craig went limp. His arms dangled at his side. It wasn't until he tossed the gun back into the armoire that Tony released him, letting Craig sit back down by the window.

Attempting to console Craig, Tony launched into a monolog speaking softly in a voice jumbled by alcohol. "We don't make the rules for Callan Park, mate. We're just bustin' our bums there to make a quid. We're ordinary workin stiffs like yourself. These things just ain't right, all buggered up. Who's made it so's you're the one to get sent

43

up and we're the bludgers sportin' uniforms? This world's crook, mate, but it don't mean us blokes are out to get ya down. I know how ya feel, I really do. My ol' man was one mean ol' bastard. You got to do what you got to do. Got to live with it. Sorry bout takin you down, but guns ain't the way to go. I reckon we're drinkin' mates. Don't have cause to do you no harm. Only thing we're thinkin' is we're your mates. Can't stay mad at your drinkin' mates, fair dinkum. Give us a go, hey?

Craig seemed to have calmed down somewhat as he sat there in silence. He looked like he was thinking more about what Tony had just done to him than what Tony was saying. At least, Tony was between Craig and the armoire.

"No worries, to hell with all this shite, com'on, let's go get some grub. There's a late night fish-n-chips joint round the corner," Craig said with a surprising new burst of enthusiasm.

I had taken advantage of the moments of calm to stretch out on the bed and soothe my dizziness. Keeping quiet, I focused my attention on the long narrow window that led to the courtyard. It was half open. It looked inviting, big enough for me to crawl through. I continued to lie motionless hoping that just maybe they would forget I was there.

"You comin'?" they both asked me at the same time.

"No, feelin' drunk… tired… no eatin'… just rest." Craig switched off the light. The door swung open and shut. I could hear Craig locking the dead bolt. I watched their shapes silhouetted on the floor as they walked under the streetlamp passing the room's lofty French windows.

A sense of relief came over me. It was time to get the hell out of there. Fearing they would notice me if I attempted to break open the front door, I scrambled to my feet, stood on the bed and flung the narrow window wide open. It was just big enough for me to squirm through and drop to the inner courtyard. I found a back gate that led to an alley.

44

Taking the direction opposite that which Tony and Craig chose, I walked down the alley to a street a block away.

For good measure, I walked a few more blocks in the direction leading away from the room, before attempting to hitch a ride back to Bondi Junction. It was around midnight, which meant few cars were on the road. Luck would have it that a man headed home from his swing shift job stopped to pick me up. I only had to walk about a half mile to get back to our flat.

When we met at Callan Park the next week, I was feeling a little guilty about leaving Tony to fend for himself. After my apologies, he told me that I had done the right thing. They never made it to the fish and chips stand. Only a few blocks down the dark street, our wild man had jumped Tony again. This time he got the best of Tony, knocking him around and throwing him down in an alley. He made off with Tony's wallet. Tony had recovered a short while later with no serious injuries. Unfortunately, or maybe fortunately, he could not find his assailant again. Tony said he was so drunk that he was not even able to find his way back to the psycho's room. I wondered just how badly he wanted to find that place, that room with the gun in it.

The crazy man never turned up again. Maybe he left Sydney. Maybe he was still out there, roaming the King's Cross looking for new victims. All I know is that I am very glad to have gotten out of that room unharmed. From that day forward, I took care to change out of my uniform before a night on the town.

Kindness, Cruelty and Death in the Asylum

The first time I saw a dead person was not at Callan Park. The body stretched out on the bed lay in a room near Chester's apartment. The man looked old to me, maybe fifty or even sixty. It was my friend Chester who called me over from his kitchen. "Want to see a dead body?" He signaled to me, his arm stretched out straight behind him with his right hand waving downward from the wrist.

We slipped quietly through the open door of his neighbors room just across the hall to see a man fully dressed, lying flat on his back on a twin bed. All the color was drained from his face and hands. His skin, a whitish grey, looked pasty like make-up had been applied to its surface. He appeared to simply be sleeping. Curiously, this spectacle did not frighten me. A hollow feeling came over me. It was the silence, the knowledge that life had abandoned this ordinary looking person. I could imagine myself lying there motionless one day, seeming to be asleep. This confusing image of things not being quite as they appeared became imprinted on my memory. That lack of life where life should have been could never be set right in my mind. This vision made being alive feel ambiguous.

The dying I witnessed at Callan Park happened over a few weeks and was more personal. It began during my assignment to the medical ward. During my first week there, our activities involved dealing with mundane problems. A handful of patients from other wards passed through for treatment of colds or flu symptoms. Some showed up with cuts, bruises or the occasional broken bone acquired during an altercation with other patients or nurses. They were quickly patched up and sent back to their wards. As my duties expanded, I assisted in the treatment of several more serious health problems that brought home the ravages of physical suffering. The sick lined up daily.

It was this resident crowd that bothered me. Every day the line formed in front of the pharmacy door. These patients had dreadful wounds covered in puss and infections every shade of purple and red that seemed to never heal. I dreaded being assigned to turn the very sick in their beds. The hospital's cloth facemasks failed to block out that sweet-rancid odor of bedsores that would form on these patients no longer able to move.

Most disturbing to me was the caring for "Vegetable Man" as the nurses called him. Vegetable Man was in the advanced stages of Parkinson's disease. A nervous system run wild had taken over his body leaving him a bundle of tensed up muscles and bones. All day long he lay in a fetal position on his side in continuous convulsions, his legs and arms rapidly jerking back and forth. The nurses laid him on a bed sheet and dragged him out onto the lawn. He writhed non-stop, crumpling up the sheet, moving grass and earth aside as if digging his own grave. They fed him by mixing the separate dishes; breads, main course and desert together in a metal bowl. Then the nurses placed the bowl near his face. He struggled to eat this mush, splattering his food all over his face and in the dirt. Afterwards, the nurses washed him down with a garden hose. In the evening they dragged him back inside on the dirty wet sheet.

One morning, I arrived to discover Vegetable Man curled up on the lawn. He lay still, dead. Chester and I were assigned the task of taking him up the hill to the morgue. Since there was nothing else available, we wrapped him in an old sheet. With me on one end and Chester on the other, we struggled to carry him up the grassy slope, forced to stop periodically under the weight. For a man who seemed so withered away, the burden of moving his corpse surprised me. His rigid limbs could not be untangled. We bore more than the weight of a stiff body. His shattered soul trapped in that web of twisted nerve endings and interlocked muscle fiber seemed to be struggling to escape from the wreckage. It tugged at the sheet's edges. While I gripped tightly, I thought I felt his spirit creep into my arms. As his fleeting soul sailed away, Vegetable Man's legacy to the living was the sensation it left imprinted in my arm. I never forgot its pull.

No family member came to see him. The nurses expressed relief at not having to feed him anymore. A week later, no one mentioned him, as if he had never existed. I remembered him clearly. I could feel his presence like a weight tugging at my arm. It still bothers me that his troubled exit from this world went almost unnoticed, as if no one dared think about his suffering.

Cruelty to patients was common among a small segment of the nurses at Callan Park. This job appealed to that element of society looking to exploit the weak or mentally feeble. My first week on night shift, I teamed with Nick, one such nurse. More of a thug than a caregiver, Nick scared me as much as he did the patients. Even though he held the position of senior nurse, he was lazy, dumb and vicious. He gave me the impression that the world existed only to satisfy his needs, or else face his wrath.

Unfortunately for one of our patients, Nick was in charge the night of a particularly bad psychotic episode. The patient began to howl and moan continuously in his closed room preventing anyone within earshot from sleeping. Since the primary perk of night shift was to be able to sleep through most of it, our patient was a thorn in Nick's side. He told me, "Don't worry, I'll take care of this". A rage burned in Nicks' eyes.

We went to the medicine cabinet. Nick unlocked it and took out the bottle of Thorazine. Routinely, our patients were given twenty milligrams of this anti-psychotic tranquilizer to calm them. In extreme cases, two hundred milligrams doses were dished out to further sedate them. Nick filled a glass with a few thousand mg of Thorazine.

We walked over to the observation cell where our patient paced about in lock-down. Nick handed me the drinking glass and told me to wait there. He went into the padded room closing the door behind him. I heard growls and loud thumps accompanied by groans of pain. Nick reappeared at the door. He took the glass in his fist. Fixing the liquid with his dead eyes, Nick re-entered the room. This time he left the door open. "Drink this!" was followed by the sound of swallowing. We returned to the nurse's station and slept through the rest of the night in silence.

At the end of my week on night shift, I had a wild idea. Being of a curious and experimental nature, I decided to discover the effect of Thorazine on the human body. After all, we dished it out to many patients on a daily bases. So I took a small amount in a flask home at the end of my Friday shift. Switching from night shift to working days the next week required some adjusting and additional rest anyway. Sitting on my bed in the front room that Saturday morning, I filled a tablespoon with Thorazine and gulped it down as if it were cough syrup. I cleared my throat with a beer while recording the deed in my journal.

The entry describes me getting groggy, my lips going numb. Then the blurred handwriting reads, "Having difficulty moving, not able to think clearly... lying down". The next journal entry took place some thirty hours later on Sunday afternoon. This writing said something about feeling exhausted and wondering what happened to Saturday, Saturday night and Sunday morning. From then on, the dull expression on so many patients' faces made perfect sense to me.

The therapy program for mental illness at Callan Park must have been inspired by the Ford Motor Company's assembly line technique. Frequently, patients complained about the lack of counseling. Yet everyone knew exactly when they would get that desperately needed help. With the exception of the emergency ward, it was quite predictable.

On Wednesdays, we nurses would line the patients up around the ward's inner courtyard. Anywhere from thirty to fifty souls gathered in a long single-file loop around the yard. Some sat, others stood, but all waited impatiently facing center court. Precisely on the hour, a team of two psychiatrists marched through the doors pushing a cart. They moved quickly around the courtyard from patient to patient.

The first doctor administered verbal treatment that went something like, "How are you feeling today, any change? Good lad, keep working on things." The second doctor conferred with the first for a minute or two, then placed a small pile of pills in the patient's hand and gave him a paper cup filled with water. Both doctors watched to assure that each patient took their pills. Then the team moved quickly to the next patient and the next. I could see they had become quite efficient at this, completing the journey around the yard while attending to all the patients in less than two hours. The hustle and bustle of this spectacle conjured up visions of Alice and the Mad Hatter's Tea Party. One could only wonder for what important date were these doctors late?

It was the children, more than any patients in the asylum that touched my heart. They were kept on a small island located in the middle of the Parramatta River a half mile off shore from the main hospital. My first ride out to our Pitt & Million Complex on the ferry barge felt like leaving civilization for the underworld. The nurses called this complex "The Island."

Mentally troubled children lived here hidden away from society in a somber stone building. This dark citadel surrounded by water offered little hope for the future. Youth housed here rode a wave of need. Wherever I walked, little hands reached out for my shirt and little eyes smiled up at me pleadingly, little feet scurried around behind me. Separated from, or abandoned by their families, they groped desperately for love and attention. They seemed so defenseless. These kids who bore labels like "Mongolian idiot" or "severely retarded" were full of energy and curiosity. They were not free to leave the island and explore the world beyond its shores. I left the place feeling sad for them.

At least the nurses working on the island appeared dedicated to caring for the children. They spoke to them in loving voices and did not chastise them for their erratic behavior.

The head nurse explained to me that corporal discipline was never used. The nurses got the children involved in games, crafts and other activities. Callan Park did have many kind-hearted nurses among the staff.

What I Didn't Learn from Australian Women

Most of my knowledge about relationships during my upbringing came from watching "Father Knows Best" and "Leave It to Beaver" on TV. Sex was a taboo subject in our house. The fact that almost my entire childhood was spent among boys didn't help. Fantasizing about Annette Funicello or sneaking peeks at the girly magazines in the tobacco shops accounted for a lot of what I expected from sex. The big deal in high school was going to the drive-in and kissing in the back seat. Our small group of outcasts did that a few times, but the girls always seemed to disappear after those movie nights. Maybe it was because I could never think of anything to say to my date after the kissing.

Once in high school, a not-quite girlfriend and I parked in a secluded spot in the high desert. We took off all our clothes. I lay on top of her pressing against her smooth flesh. She felt great and we kissed for a long while. Not quite sure what we should do next, both of us got confused. We put our clothes back on. I drove her home to the trailer park where she served me some ice tea.

My advanced training began aboard the *Cap Finisterre*. The German sailors liked whores. They spoke of love for sale with a nonchalant attitude like it was good wholesome fun. One night, shortly after my arrival in Sydney I figured I'd saved up a few quid to blow on a frivolous adventure.

After the pubs closed, I decided to take the next logical step in my sex education. A few of us drinking buddies headed towards the docks to pay Sydney's red light district a visit. Drunk enough to get up the nerve, I surveyed the available ladies and chose an ordinary looking prostitute.

51

Her voice sounded kind, not too intimidating. She was not beautiful enough to be intimidating.

I had learned from listening to the sailor stories that I had to pay in cash up front. We entered a small drab room that was almost empty. A dingy curtain with dull red strips hung over the window. The room was dark. On a twin bed pushed up against one wall lay a mattress covered with a worn sheet. It looked dirty, uninviting. The iron box springs, visible under the mattress, surely creaked. A little square stand in the corner held a washbasin and a bar of soap. Beyond it, an interior door closed off the room. There was no provision for romance here.

The woman took me over to the washstand, had me drop my drawers, and gave me a clinical wash. Her touch lacked passion. After a careful examination of my 'instrument' for signs of disease, she marched me over to the small bed. She plopped down on her back, pulled up her dress and spread her legs, offering her exposed bottom, open for business. Her expression of impatience signaled me to hurry up. I felt uncomfortable, unromantic, nervous, drunk, and wanted to leave. None-the-less my desire for sex expelled any thoughts of escape, driving me on top of her. Confusion raged in my head. Blood pumping, hips rocking, I pounded away trying to achieve some relief. The conflict between my emotions and my libido was blocking the ability to climax. After what seemed a very short time, the whore slapped me on the bottom exclaiming, "Time's up". I needed more quarters to put in the slot, if I wanted to keep riding. My wallet was empty.

"No, no, I'm not done. It takes me a while, just a little longer." I pleaded. This bought me a little more time, not nearly enough. Then the call came that really set me on guard.

"Hey Mack, this guy won't get off," she yelled.

In response, a scary sounding male voice growled through the interior door. "You want me to come deal with him?"

Smothering my unfulfilled desire, the left-brain asserted control and I climbed off, still complaining I hadn't finished.

"Look love, this is me busiest time, come back later and you can have another go."

Maybe all was not lost. I decided to hang around for a few more hours and try again later. Sure enough, good to her word, the prostitute invited me in for a second round. Wouldn't you know it! The second visit was an exact repeat of the first culminating in the same expulsion and dissatisfaction.

This experience in soliciting the services of a prostitute became my last. I found this kind of sex to be all too spiritless, squalid, and humiliating. The sailors neglected to warn that entering certain rooms can put their visitors at risk of being transported to a nightmarish corner of the Twilight Zone.

Unsatisfied with love for sale, I returned to a less controversial way of meeting women, during the day in a public place. It was downtown Sydney on a clear day that I first spotted Maureen. A smartly dressed young lady, she possessed a gracious manner that I captured my eye and pricked my imagination. When first I approached this lovely miss all that came out was, "Hi, my name's Richard."

Actually, it took courage to force those words from my lips considering it was midday in a respectable part of town and I was sober. Her reply took me by surprise. "Don't worry, I won't tell anyone." She responded in a jokingly cynical tone. This was not going to be an easy connection to make.

We started our meeting during her lunch break from the bank where she worked as a teller. Maureen was an expert shopper and knew central Sydney's boutique district well. Our conversations revolved around Maureen's vision of social identity. Mostly, I listened as she educated me during the excursions through all sorts of stores. Furniture

53

went beyond its functional uses to become items of distinction. Differences in colors and fabrics represented ascending levels of success and good taste. Interior design and gardening played a far more important role in life than I had ever imagined. I discovered that ignoring those irritating springs struggling to poke through the couch's cushions back at our bachelor pad could result in a serious drop down a few rungs on the ladder of social standing.

Maureen represented a high point of sorts for my interactions with Australian females. She raised my understanding of a "normal" relationship with the opposite sex to its highest level so far. Maureen created a vision of Australian life previously unknown to me. Her confident lectures on etiquette filled me with self-doubt. How could I have ignored all the obvious signs around me? Maureen painted a detailed vision of the meaning of propriety. Holding me by the hand, she boldly led me towards a complex, if somewhat intimidating, world of friends, civil conversation and a veiled promise of happiness. All this and I loved her firm slender body. The pearly gates were swinging open.

Just as success approached, mysterious barriers popped up. The door to Maureen's passionate side appeared to be locked or at least jammed shut. Every time I slid my hand across her backside and tried to kiss her, she pulled away.

A transformation in my appearance was mandatory before I would be allowed to approach her inner sanctum. Maureen bravely faced this challenge head-on, escorting me to men's clothing and shoe stores. Wouldn't that nice suit look good on me? How chic I would be in those slick Italian shoes! In secret, I cringed at the prospect of those narrow Italian shoes on my big fat feet. Regardless, her minimum standards must be met before our social contract could be sealed.

Maybe it was the Italian shoes, but more likely it was the experience of our date to a jazz club that pushed me over the edge. Even though none of my mates changed out of their jeans and tee shirts to go to the pub, I was prepared to put on a clean shirt and shave if it made Maureen happy. Even though there was no way those narrow Italian shoes would last a day on my feet without causing blisters, I wished I could wear them for her.

But, jazz carried the rhythms of the soul. It conjured up the spirits of my Beatnik gods. That night we spent drinking wine and hanging out at one of Sydney's better jazz clubs, I thought for sure she would become intoxicated with the sounds of undulating passion. We would ride on the silky wave of Miles Davis right through her bedroom door.

Unfortunately, a disapproving Maureen brooded over her wine and complained about this irritating music. She expressed relief when we finally left the club. Such surroundings held no place in her vision of a wholesome Australian life. The road to better living lay elsewhere.

I politely escorted Maureen back to the path of her choosing. I bid a mournful farewell to that lovely figure of hers. My chance to join Sydney's better crowd wilted away as she wiggled her cute behind up the steps that night locking the door behind her.

A few months later a very different sort of woman came into my life. It was during my quest for the 'cool scene' that fate drew Sonia to me at The Brass Lantern. It had taken a while to locate this Beatnik pub in the conservative atmosphere of Sydney. Only a few blocks from the harbor, an atmosphere of transience hung over the place. Blacks and whites mingled as people drifted in and out. This crowd dressed like those San Francisco beats I so admired. Jazz and corduroy filled its narrow hall. Sonia noticed me eyeing her from across the smoky bar as I downed a few pints.

The opposite of Maureen, her curvaceous body warmly beckoned. Her soft pale flesh was draped in a colorful flowing sheer dress. She wore magical black leather boots. Sonia's big dark eyes let off occasional sparks in my direction. She excelled in the art of flirtation. This was going to be an easy connection.

We must have talked about something. Verbal exchanges got lost in the exotic odor of her perfume, in the hypnotic pull of her sultry eyes and in her body brushing discretely against mine. As we left the pub together, I clung to her side prancing along like a puppy anticipating its treat. We snuggled together on the ferry ride across the harbor to Manly Bay where she lived. The thought of entering her bedroom sweetened the moonlight ride over the gently rolling waves. At last the erotic adventure I dreamed about was coming true.

Sonia lived in a pleasant room on a quiet street overlooking the bay. It felt feminine with colorful fabrics, make-up bottles and exciting looking garments scattered around. The situation seemed promising and my spirits were high until the knock came at the door. A pair of syrupy male voices called out through the locked door.

"Sonia, it's us darling. We're ready. Can we come in now?" they called out with testosterone driven urgency.

I recognized the sound of wolves using sheepish tones. Gesturing to Sonia with my arms not to open the door and stay quiet made no impression on her. She seemed excited by their presence. Those dark eyes began to glow anew. After giving me a sweet smile that left me confused and fearful, she turned and opened the door a crack.

Seeing me in the room did not deter these guys in the slightest. They continued to plead with Sonia to let them in. My body started to go into flight or fight mode. To my amazement, Sonia went into the hall leaving the door open behind her. I heard her speaking in sexually rich tones; watched her float out the door flowing across the hall in a wave of hair and lace. Magically, Sonia conjured up a spell casting it over these dazed young men. She guided the pair down the hall, out the entry and into the night. I had greatly underestimated the power of her feminine allure. She triumphantly returned, ready to deal with me.

Our dance of love started out on a strange note. "You're a virgin aren't you?" She observed with an all-knowing lustful inflection.

What constituted a virgin? I wondered. I knew all the sailors tales, had been with a whore, and reached a respectable understanding of the physical mechanics. Was climaxing technically a mandatory part of this equation? My lack of response excited her.

Sonia undressed and got under the sheets quickly. I didn't get to see much of her body as I hastily undressed and followed. While we lay side by side, she reached between my legs and grabbed my penis. Oh boy, this was going to be it. Sonia's elated voice bounced around in my head making no sense. All my focus was on her hand around my penis.

She was squeezing with all her might. Even though it only mildly hurt, I was sure this went beyond stimulation. It felt like an act filled with rage exacting some tormented revenge against a painful past. Not knowing how to react, I tossed about half-heartedly and said nothing. We rolled around the bed for a long while. I struggled to position myself between her legs. At times she cooperated, at others she crushed away with her hands or thighs. Sonia's aroused squeals and squeaks made it clear she was enjoying this wrestling match. Eventually, I climaxed somewhere between her legs and fell asleep at her side.

The next morning, I woke up sore, but contented. We had coffee and biscuits together. Sonia continued to talk provocatively about my sexual education. Nothing sunk in. I tried to grasp what had happened the night before. Was I still a virgin? Who were those guys at the door? What kind of sexual education had Sonia received?

She was just too much for me to keep up with and we both knew it. After an amicable parting, I strolled down to the docked ferryboat with the sun on my back and a beautiful view of the bay. I felt relieved, yet puzzled, by this odd romp in the hay with such a passionate wrestler.

A Winter's Farewell

With the arrival of fall things began to change. Dwayne bought a motorcycle in late May. One rainy night after a heated argument with his girlfriend, he hopped on the motorcycle and raced from her apartment in a rage. He was not wearing a helmet or protective clothing. Speeding around a corner, he lost control; the bike skidding to the ground. The bike began to slide on its side, and plowed head-on, into a stone wall.

After six weeks in the hospital with wires holding his head together, Dwayne was released into the welcoming arms of his girlfriend. In light of his fragile state, he quit Callan Park to take a job as a teller in the Bank of Australia. Dwayne started to spend most of his evenings at his young lady's flat.

Another member of our small circle of friends and fellow nurse, Chester also went his own way. The problem he faced was termination from Callan Park any day. We discovered his secret one afternoon at his apartment overlooking King's Cross. Standing on the little balcony enjoying the view, Chester suddenly stumbled to the carpet and went into convulsions. I thought he was having a heart attack, but Dwayne recognized the symptoms. "It's an epileptic fit." He called out, "Bring me a kitchen spoon"

Dwayne shoved the spoon in Chester's mouth while I held his head. A trickle of blood ran across the spoon. Dwayne claimed this was necessary to prevent Chester from choking on his own tongue, even if it meant cutting his mouth. After three or four minutes, Chester calmed down regaining consciousness. He looked really worried. "You can't tell anyone about this! Please don't tell anyone. If Callan Park finds out, they'll fire me!"

58

Apart from being epileptic, Chester was Filipino which placed him even further at the margins of Australian society than me. I had little doubt they were going to fire him. It was only a matter of time. He withdrew from our little band of friends becoming something of a loner after this incident. Chester's flat, our King's Cross hangout, was no longer available.

In late-May the rain began to fall. This rain differed from that light California variety or even those heavy thunderstorms that announced the arrival of spring during my childhood back in Ohio and Tennessee. The gods poured water down on Sydney with a density like that of our bathroom shower. This monsoon-like rainfall pounded the city non-stop for days even though we were some thirty degrees south of the equator.

Those expansive summer evenings we had shared in lively discussions so full of humor at the Sydney pubs transformed into drenched nights of senseless drinking in claustrophobic bars. I began to dread the morning-after headaches. While my closest friends were all undergoing changes in their lives, I became restless. Thoughts of moving south to Melbourne came to mind.

I decided to take a French class. My mother had minored in French in college. She often talked about France as if it were a magical place. The time felt right to look to a future across the oceans. Our little French lesson book had a multi-shaded green map of France just inside the front jacket. In a highly scientific approach, I drew an 'x' through the map. The town at the center of my 'X' bore the name of Dijon. Being in the middle of France, Dijon must be the place where people spoke perfect French. I decided to go there.

This time I knew how to find a ship and visited the docks regularly throughout June including visits to the offices of the Matson Lines, my former employer's affiliate. Apparently, that messy little mishap with the Master Cook never reached my personnel file. In late June, they sent me to see the captain of the Gustav Pistor, a rickety old bucket of bolts headed back to the scrap heaps of Germany on its final voyage.

The captain, a friendly fellow, stood ready to take on some free help. The *Gustav Pistor* badly needed maintenance and I was offered the job of painting the ship from bow to stern, a major task for this ten-ton freighter. Fortunately, there would be plenty of time since her journey covered half the globe. The planned route took her around the Cape of Australia, over the Indian Ocean, up the Suez Canal, east through the Mediterranean past Gibraltar, up the English Channel, across the North Sea following the Elbe River down to Hamburg, a three month journey.

CHAPTER THREE
Crossing Zero, Moving North

Melbourne

A chilling breeze cut across the deck as the *Gustav Pistor* turned imperceptibly in the misty air. Grey clouds heavy with rain drifted overhead. Tug boats had been slowly towing her around to face seaward for most of the morning. Sydney's jagged skyline silhouetted beyond the crowded docks formed a melancholy panorama destined to disappear from view before nightfall. I leaned against the ship's steel railing, taking a final survey of this extraordinary place, which had been my home for the past year. Blasts of cold air pierced my cotton jacket. My cheeks grew red. The moment felt right for a solitary farewell.

I thought of the people whose lives I had briefly shared, our relationships full of twists and turns. It seemed unlikely that we would ever see one another again. No one came to the docks as none of us cared much for goodbyes. Alone at the stern, I felt a little piece of myself stranded across the harbor. Icy waters cut off any further access to this world from which we slowly pulled away. A shiver ran up my spine yanking my attention back to the present, reminding me that the time had come to look to the future. Doing an about face, I walked back towards mid ship. Making a fresh start with no awkward mishaps to overcome made for a good beginning.

This time I felt confident, just another sailor as far as the rest of the crew was concerned. The captain assigned me to a cabin one deck below the mess hall. My new German roommate had a name so hard to pronounce that he called himself "Joe". A long wiry character some ten years my senior, he looked so much the classic sailor that he could easily have blended in aboard a seventeenth century schooner.

We settled into comfortable terms from that first day. An understanding was quickly established. Conversation would be limited to general subjects such as food, beer and Germany. We respected the shared space. I had learned from living in Dwayne's crowded front room that it was best to keep things simple when people are forced to share a very small space for a long time.

Never the less, it didn't take long to discover a few of Joe's irritating qualities. He insisted on leaving the portal open even in bad weather, so great was his need for fresh air. One particularly rough night, the sea rushed in soaking all my belongings, almost destroying my diary. Other times, it was just damned cold.

In spite of a few annoying habits, Joe had his good points. He kept his space tidy. Rising every morning at seven a.m. to shave, he always cleaned our small sink afterwards. Joe folded his clothes, neatly storing them in his locker every evening. With precise repetition, his daily routines were carried out like mantras. These rituals of cleaning himself, washing his things or folding clothes provided some comfort as our small ship tossed about, surrounded by a vastly powerful and unpredictable ocean.

We headed west, traveling a few miles off shore. Then turning south, we set course for Melbourne keeping the coastline just within view. The sea proved to be much rougher for this short jaunt between the two cities than it had been when crossing the Pacific. My stomach began to churn. I lost my appetite. It came as a great relief when we tied up to the dock in Melbourne's small harbor.

The long awaited visit to this city, often in my thoughts back in Sydney, was something of a letdown. The authorities strictly enforced curfews. With no sailor's bars or private clubs that stayed open after ten o'clock anywhere near, the city transformed into a ghost town shortly after sunset. We were all relieved when, a few days into our stay, the crew received an invitation from a local maritime society to attend a presentation on Alice Springs.

A bunch of us trekked up concrete sidewalks between darkened buildings on a windy night until reaching the only lighted storefront in sight. Inside the small hall, a few rows of grey metal folding chairs were set up on a creaky wooden floor. A black electrical cord split the rows right down the middle. There were no decorations on the walls of this hall. In the back center, a brown metal slide projector, its carousel filled with slides, stood ready on a card table. Center forward, a four foot crystalline white panel extended out of a retractable screen case. Supported by a steel tripod, it rose up like an abandoned billboard. A few grey haired men talked softly while waiting for everyone to be seated. Finally, the room darkened around a single beam of light glaring against the white screen. Large glowing pictures began to appear. From the back of the room, a man launched excitedly into his presentation in fatherly tones. His voice suggested a great adventure.

At first, this small Australian hamlet of Alice Springs surrounded by an immense red desert, appeared charming. Soon, we realized that this was a very small town in the middle of nowhere. The narrator's enthusiasm over his trip to this dusty outback contrasted sharply with the images. He believed himself to have taken a wondrous journey. He rambled on, out of touch with his audience. Before him sat a group of seasoned sailors, men who had circled the globe for years traveling every corner of the seven seas. Did this man really think he could capture the interest of such salty dogs with pictures of sheep farmers and tractors?

The evening would have been a complete loss had not been for the late arrival of a beautiful young blonde woman. She sported a stylishly cut outfit with its well-fitting mohair sweater and a short skirt revealing some lovely long legs.

All eyes were on those legs glowing in the lamplight. Alice Springs dwindled to a flickering blur washing over her thighs. The hungry hounds had gotten a whiff of the fox and her sentinels sensed the danger. They whisked her off to safety the moment the show ended. Our trip to Alice Springs faded to a sullen close leaving only the bleak walk through icy winds back to the ship.

For most of the six days we were tied up in Melbourne, staying onboard afforded no more comfort than going ashore. The ship was taking on bails of wool. Crane's swung pallets of the loosely bundled material into the hulls all day long. Itchy particles filled the air. A joyous relief rambled through the ship the afternoon we finally closed our hatches, pulled up anchor, and headed out to sea.

Through the Bight
The *Gustav Pistor* tumbled head-on into icy currents coming up from the South Pole. Our route took us through the Great Australian Bight. This often rough stretch of ocean tossed our ship around like a leaf in the wind. We had the misfortune of running into a storm in this very region of ocean where many a vessel that went before us had been swallowed by the sea. My seasickness became so bad that I could no longer stand. For days, the nausea plagued me. I periodically hung over the edge of my bunk and threw up into a bucket. Every morning, the third mate came, angry and yelling, indifferent to my condition, to rouse me from my bed for work.

One day, when the third mate didn't show up to fetch me, I struggled out of bed and up to the main deck. Hanging onto the cabin door, I peeked out to see what caused all the seesawing. Suddenly, my body jerked forward. Looking down along the deck, I saw the front of the ship plunge downward, disappearing into a wall of seawater and foam. Abruptly thrown back, I gripped the doorknob in both hands with all my might as a thundering mountain of salt water crashed down over the cabin. Quickly returning to my bunk, I braced myself and prayed we didn't go down to Davy Jones's locker. The third mate be damned!

Finally, as we moved beyond Perth into the Indian Ocean, the sea calmed, and I returned to my task of chipping away at the chunks of grey paint that flaked off the rusty steel deck. Each day the sea became calmer until one day all the waves mysteriously disappeared. For the next six weeks, we slid forward on a waveless sheet of blue. A pleasantly warm sun rose in the sky each morning. Shirts came off and tans appeared on everyone as we settled back into our routines.

My new friend Gunter, a quiet young man who did not read books and barely spoke English, would challenge me to a game of chess each evening after dinner. It started out with an easy win for Gunter. Over the next weeks, I improved to the point that I once almost beat Gunter. Even with time, my chess skills never became good enough for me to win. More importantly, I learned not to be as arrogant or foolish as to underestimate the skills of an opponent based on appearances or background.

I was the assistant to the chief paint chipper and cable greaser. The main benefit of this easy job was that I had someone to goof off with all day. We joked around a lot. He tried to convince me that when we crossed the equator, if I went to pee with the wind, my pee would reverse on me. We got a few laughs and some mileage out of dumb jokes like that one.

Mostly, I did a lot of contemplating and reassessing. Much like my first sea voyage, I had a lot of time to myself. Just as during that first journey, every evening around sunset, I sat at the bow of the ship to dream, remember and find peace, to evolve.

It was a trouble free trip for the most part. With the exception of a small incident between the cook's mess boy and me. Maybe it was because I had let my hair grow longer than most in an attempt to emulate my Beatnik heroes.

This cabin boy decided that I must be gay. At first, my mates passed on to me the rumors he had started. Then he got bolder, giving me sly glances and crafty smiles. One day after lunch I caught sight of him out of the corner of my eye. He was whispering to the cook something noticeably nasty while looking directly at me, a smirk glistening across his lips. By this time, I had toughened up. Pacifism had become a relative value for me and his current behavior fell outside of my new guidelines.

Angry, I walked over to him in a sufficiently threatening way to inspire the cook to step aside. The mess boy was short. I had to bend to grab him by the calves, lift his body up and hang him partially over the side. As he swung over the edge dangling above the waves, he looked terrified. I told him if I heard he was talking about me again that I would throw him overboard. The rest of the crew must have understood my motives, no one interfered. That put an end to his malicious behavior.

This journey was so long that it went beyond losing contact with the world. The *Gustav Pistor* became the world. When the engine broke down in the middle of the Indian Ocean, it presented a serious problem. With no waves, we just sat there wondering how long the food would last. To this day, I wonder if radio communications with shore would have been possible. Not to worry though. Thanks to our skilled German mechanics and a storeroom of spare parts we were up and running again in a few days.

Our first stop to refuel, after many weeks at sea, was the Port of Aden in Yemen. An exotic, but squalid place, both the air and water were heavily polluted. It must have been a troubled city as the ship did not dock and the crew had strict orders to stay onboard. Strange music that sounded like the howling of dusty desert winds filled the air. Long high-pitched moaning chants reached our ears from the towering sand colored mosques across the bay.

A few shoddy harbor vessels tied up to us. Their crew came aboard with big transistor radios, souvenirs, and colorful clothes to sell. One fellow in jeans and a grubby shirt walked up to me and asked if I would like to buy some pictures. He handed me a crude black and white photo of a naked woman on all fours being mounted by a big dog. I could not believe what I was seeing. Repulsed, I quickly moved away from him, but that image troubled me for years. No wonder our captain refused to dock or allow anyone ashore.

The day after we left Aden, a new stretch of arid coast appeared on the horizon. None of the sailors got too excited since we weren't going ashore. For me, however, it was a wondrous sight like the surface of another planet. Miles of rolling sand dunes came into view and passed as we followed along the coast of Egypt. Periodically, camels trod along dusty costal roads. Patches of greenery and palm trees rose out of sandy estuaries marking isolated coastal villages. Water buffalo turned circles around wooden milling wheels driven by men in hooded cloaks. Those same haunting high-pitched chants drifted on the morning and evening winds. The sea narrowed to an artery as we entered the Suez Canal.

After months floating on the open ocean, it seemed like an illusion to be surrounded by sand. We ambled along some twenty feet above the earth with the desert just a stone's throw away. This narrow channel of water carried us towards the Mediterranean. We passed small groups of shrouded men walking the dirt trails. Others tilled the few fields scattered along the canal. They looked like characters from the Bible guiding wooden handled v-shaped plows pulled by oxen.

The only distraction to all this wonder was my eccentric roommate, Joe, who had stopped talking to me. He told me that he did not want me to "find out what in my brain." If I attempted to be friendly, he replied, "You try to sell me for stupid or something" Up to more odd antics; he refused to turn the fan on during the hot nights. When I had to pass gas one evening, he called me "all rotten inside." He should have turned on the fan.

Our ship rocked with a gentle steady movement as we left Egypt and set out across the Mediterranean. Dolphins followed the ship for a few days off the coast of Greece under beautiful blue skies and pristine waters. After a long stretch of open sea, Gibraltar came into view early one morning. We passed under the shadow of this colossal wall of solid rock bound for rougher seas.

Heading north, the English Channel tossed us about and a touch of my seasickness returned. It was allayed by the new wave of excitement that ran through the ship. This last leg of our journey would lead down the Elbe River and back to the homeland of my fellow sailors.
Gliding down the Elbe introduced me to Europe for the first time. As the estuary narrowed, rolling hills came into view, covered with dark trees and deep undergrowth. A grey mist enveloped this imposing, almost hostile, world. The lush greens and bright yellows of the tropics had made me want to tumble into their warmth. This was another kind of green. This was the somber green of a defiant forest with black barked trees and thick foliage, layers of dead leaves and rotting branches discouraged passage. Here stood a forest loath to reveal its well kept secrets. One could easily imagine men, caught behind its curtain on a black winter solstice, turning into wolves.

The Port of Hamburg

It took a day to make our way down the Elbe to Hamburg.
As we approached the city, the forest softened into a more
welcoming woodland. Roads wound in and out of the
trees. Occasionally, a captivating village peeked out from a
cove at the mouth of a stream. Dwellings painted in pale
yellows and browns with pointed stone roofs rose from the
clearing. Cobblestone streets wound through the homes
and buildings. These boroughs were even more beautiful
than the pictures I had seen in Life Magazine, always
available on our living room coffee table back home.

Soon the river narrowed. The *Gustav Pistor* moved closer
to shore. We traveled out of the main shipping lanes yielding too much larger freighters that passed us only yards
away. The river became a liquid highway with two lanes of
ships moving in each direction. Its water turned from a
brown to a foul grayish color. Debris floated helter skelter
on its surface. Our old freighter chugged along, reduced to
a broken old sparrow, limping home among the hulking
hawks and buzzards of industry.

As we approached Hamburg, palatial homes began to pep-
per the landscape. These expansive dwellings sprawled
across the hillsides. Their white terraces and wooden staircases led down hillsides to private docks where yachts or
sail boats were housed. My shipmates claimed these homes
belonged to executives and industrial barons, owners of
maritime companies.

When the Elbe widened into the great seaport of Hamburg,
my confidence melted. I grew smaller and smaller as we
entered this sprawling urban landscape of bellowing
smokestacks, steel ships and long piers as far as the eye
could see. For what seemed like hours, we past dock after
dock. Cranes dominated the horizon in every direction,
forming a fence around the sky. Mooring to shore in

70

Hamburg in the damp cold of late afternoon, we entered a daunting old world. I felt more than ready to leave the seaman's life and this mammoth port behind. But, I felt apprehensive about my ability to survive on the meager savings accumulated in Australia. No one was waiting on the pier to offer me employment.

The streets next to the docks hosted modest hotels for the constant stream of sailors. I found a cheap room with a toilet down the hall and no bath, dropped off my suitcase, and went to visit the only tourist attraction I knew of in Hamburg; the one I had learned about from our crew, the Reeperbahn.

Sydney's King's Cross district was a lively nightspot, but the nightlife in the Reeperbahn district bordered on the surreal. Not far into this section of town, glittering neon signs brightened the streets as foot traffic grew in density. The crowds became almost uniquely male. Lots of big, burly men emerged drunk and staggering around. To me, they looked wild-eyed and ready to explode with incoherent rage at any moment. I came to a street blocked from view by two eight foot high concrete walls. A four foot gap between the overlapping walls allowed pedestrians to enter as one might enter a labyrinth.

Once inside, the quarter mile long passageway was full of little shop windows, one after the other. A woman sat on display in each window. Women balanced on stools wearing only negligee. Some wore red and black corseted or laced outfits while others attracted passers-by with brightly colored garter belts attached to fishnet stockings. These burlesque-like costumes and protruding flesh drew attention away from the women's blank facial expressions and glazed over eyes. I imagined disturbed souls hiding behind these brazen masquerades. Exiled spirits, personalities that no one desired to know in any depth. I certainly did not want to discover their innermost thoughts. My little whore back in Sydney now seemed sweet and innocent.

Erotic, exciting, frightening and intimidating all at once, this caldron of lust created a confusing scene. I might have struggled longer with my lustful fascinations while moving toward the exit at the far end of the street, had it not been for all the big scary drunks stumbling around. Trouble simmered just below their surface. I suspected fights were surely going to break out soon. So I returned to the hotel early that night.

With a visit to Hamburg's finer cultural sites under my belt and money tight, I needed to get to France. I managed to find the cavernous train station the next morning. Suitcase in hand, I eventually located the ticket windows. Using sign language, I purchased a one-way ticket all the way to Dijon, France. Once on board, the train rocked and creaked its way toward the French boarder.

CHAPTER FOUR
French Reconstruction

Dijon: Finding My Way

There must have been some karmic link between me and the designer of my little French lesson book. Contrary to what the 'X' on the map in my lesson book suggested, Dijon was not in the center of France. One hundred miles southeast of Paris, it occupied the heart of Burgundy not far from the foothills of the Alps. Dijon was storybook beautiful. From the moment I stepped of the train, it felt comfortable, almost familiar. I knew I was supposed to stay here.

Approaching the city, the train skirted a rocky cliff before descending through a narrow tunnel into the station. Fertile farmland blanketed the valleys, orchards scattered across the hillsides surrounded this small city. This terrain was quite different from the arid expanses, sage and rocky hills of Southern California. Still, some similarities existed that I found comforting. Dijon's population paralleled that of Riverside. Both downtown districts could be crossed on foot in fifteen minutes and people went about their business at an easy pace. The city was large enough to provide variety while the countryside lay only a short distance away.

The more I discovered Dijon, the more it seduced and fascinated me. Narrow streets twisted through the town center binding it into a web of antiquity. Store fronts were painted in moss greens and mahogany browns that framed tall glass windows. The low brass handles on shop doors were clearly designed for bygone generations. Signs stretched above the windows hand painted in intricate gold lettering over dark backgrounds recalled another century. Cathedrals, fountains, stone streets, and buildings covered in ivy seemed to appear at every turn. Arching passageways led to secluded courtyards creating magnificent visions of tranquility. Like the young man entering Brigadoon, I had stumbled, an uninvited intruder, into this mysterious realm.

74

This ancient citadel presented a new challenge. How could I fit in here? To find a place in this unfamiliar world for a blue eyed, six foot four Yankee like me became my new ambition. The people around me were short, dark haired, and brown eyed on the whole. Almost everyone dressed stylishly. Still, they gave the impression of a humorless crowd bustling about town ignoring one another in the streets. These French rarely smiled or greeted passers by. Yet, when I watched them congregating in small groups, at leisure, talking with friends, a tender affection blossomed in their expressions. I had no idea what they were saying, but their conversations filled the air with compassionate sounds. Arms swayed about and hands carved delicate gestures in harmony with the cadence of their voices. Eyes glistened and sparkled, full of caring and kindness. They shared a form of intense intimacy that I found alluring. I wanted to be a part of so much joy.

Armed with a handful of French words and lots of determination, I set about poking at the edges of this ostensibly impenetrable culture. After setting up camp in a small hotel on one of the back streets, I started hanging around "le Jardin Darcy", a charming little park just off the central square full of flowers with two spiral staircases that encircled a sea shell shaped fountain. People in the park were not in a hurry, making them approachable. My plan was to practice French by asking folks simple questions and trying to understand their responses. In just a day or two, it became pretty easy to understand what time it was, what people's names were, where the bathrooms were and that "l'eau dans la fontaine est bleu" (the water in the fountain was blue), while "les arbres sont marrons" (the trees are brown) and "l'herbe est verte" (the grass is green).

Then, one day good fortune smiled in the morning sun. My latest linguistic subject turned out to be a student at the local university. He spoke in English providing advice. If I wanted to learn French, it would be a good idea to sign up for classes at the local university. When I explained my financial constraints, he gave me the best news of all. The French government subsidized student expenses at the University of Dijon. Not only would it be almost free to enroll, I could live in the dormitories and eat at the student restaurant for very little money.

The University of Dijon administration offices were just across the square, down a side street, in one of those ivy covered stone buildings. Just as the student had said, the officials inside enrolled me in a program for foreign students for a modest fee. They received me with considerable warmth and kindness. The people working in these offices expressed a genuine curiosity about the United States which they referred to as "l'Amérique" and were pleased that I wanted to learn French. They made me feel safe and welcome.

I was issued a student card. Afterwards, I applied for a student visa in a nearby office and headed up the road to check into one of the school's dormitories. It was exhilarating to think of myself as a college student. For the first time in a long time, I felt capable, ready to succeed in life, to learn scholarly facts, read books. Anything seemed possible.

Remembering my experience at the University of Sydney, I promised to make a point of talking to any construction workers around campus that crossed my path. Instilled with the spirit of learning, I picked up a French dictionary and a book on verb conjugation along with a copy of the local paper.

The University's housing compound was a pleasant two mile walk away from the town center. The men's complex consisted of a series of five four story buildings, each lodging some 200 students. A comparable complex for the women was just down the hill around the corner.

On each floor, long hallways extended in two directions from a central elevator with private rooms on either side. Two narrow bathing areas with a half dozen shower stalls were located the end of either hall. Meeting with the building manager in "Pavillon Vauban", my new home, I paid the first month's rent.

It felt wonderful to be able to afford the rent for a month with what remained of my modest savings. Equally satisfying was to purchase a month's worth of meal tickets and still have few francs left over. The money that remained would not cover a second month.

Fortunately, classes did not begin for four weeks giving me a few extra weeks for full time work. I quickly found the university employment office downtown. Through them, I got my first opportunity to earn money in France. The office arranged for me to work the fields at "les vendanges" picking grapes for that year's wine production. My assigned vineyard was located in a village in the "Cotes des Nuits" region, less than an hour outside Dijon. The next afternoon I caught a bus to Gevrey Chambertin.

The Grape Harvest
The farm at Gevrey Chambertin, a former medieval monastery, sat on a gentle knoll. A wide iron gate opened onto a square courtyard enclosed on all four sides by moss covered stone buildings. In one corner a tractor stuck out between two tall wooden doors. The flatbed trailer attached to it disappeared into the shadows of what looked like a cavernous barn. A few chickens hopped about the courtyard next to a small fenced vegetable garden. The main farmhouse rose above the other buildings. Three stories high, it had a thick wooden door darkened by age, its shuttered windows strategically placed a good two meters above the ground limited access to the building.

77

The lady in charge, Madame Morgeot, greeted me warmly. I followed her into the barn, then through double doors that led to a large dining hall and wine cellar. Just inside, a dark wooden table some twenty feet long paralleled the outer wall. Its thick top had long flat benches tucked under either side. Nicks and marks peppered its face, tell-tale remains suggesting many years of feasting and reveling had passed over its surface.

At the far end, a staircase led up to a dormitory offering modest accommodations. Eight beds were lined up in a row, each one separated by a small night stand/cabinet. A thin mattress lay on the wooden platform of each bed covered by a sheet and one woolen blanket. The only sink in the room stood against the back wall. Next to it, a narrow door led to a small toilette. This toilette consisted of a hole leading to a drain pipe in the floor with two raised islands on either side of the hole to stand on. A white porcelain knob hung at the end of a rusty chain suspended from the ceramic bowl mounted high above. A roll of rough brown paper dangled over a wire loop nailed to the adjacent wall. The austere character of the place put me at ease. Jack Karouac would have undoubtedly approved.

My timing was excellent. I had arrived just as preparations for the evening meal were in progress. Soon the dinner bell rang and the other workers began to arrive. They were an eclectic mix of young people from Spain and Italy. The group also included another French student from Dijon. This gathering was largely made up of males However, a female French student as well as a Spanish girl counted among them. None of the workers spoke in English.

Everyone crowded onto the benches, passing bread around the table. Madame Morgeot and her daughter, Jeanine, a girl a few years younger than myself, poured wine from flasks which they periodically refilled at the oak barrels behind us.

It is amazing how quickly the mind learns critical language skills when the belly is growling. I was soon calling out to pass the bread, to fill my plate with more meat, potatoes and vegetables, and of course, to fill my glass!

Beer had been my drink of choice in Australia. Here, I discovered the wonderful wine of Gevrey Chambertin. People in this country did not drink in the manner of the Australians. Wine was a part of their daily life, a fundamental component of the main meals. These people showed no interest in getting drunk for recreational pleasure, nor did they seem to need alcohol to inspire their imaginations or ignite their passions.

As the meal progressed, a chorus of voices filled the room culminating in a cacophony of gaiety and laughter. Everyone was talking at the same time, but no one seemed to mind. The Italians around me formed a mini-convention focusing in on me. They used markedly slow speech for my benefit, pointing out utensils, foods, and dishes. It became a game of sorts. They nurtured me with words to pronounce and laughed in satisfaction at my modest successes. I felt like a puppy getting a treat every time I rolled over or shook hands. My treats were delicious plates of food, fresh baked bread, and wine served up in an atmosphere of affectionate merriment. The evening carried on like this until the flow of words slowed to a trickle, overpowered by drooping eyelids and warm bellies. After all, everyone but me had just labored ten hours in the fields.

We eight males climbed the back stairs to our rigid beds while the ladies disappeared into another part of the house. Just before sunrise, the roosters helped us out of our beds along with Monsieur Morgeot who turned on the lights. After a quick breakfast of bread and cheese washed down with a bowl of warm café au lait, we climbed on the flat-bed trailer, rubber boots dangling, and headed out for the vineyards. A short ride away, long rows of grapes awaited us in the cool dampness of a thin light at daybreak.

We carried wooden baskets with wire handles. At first, my hands were cold and the constant stooping and bending to pluck grapes made my back hurt. Finally, I adapted to the chill. A bit hungry, but mostly curious, I ate a few grapes. They were bitter-sweet and full of seeds, not all that tasty. As the sun slowly rose to warm my body, I settled into a rhythm moving gradually down the rows.

At mid morning, Jeanine came up the dirt path dressed in a modest cotton smock and tall rubber boots. She carried a bucket filled with water and a large bottle of wine. Jeanine did not strike me as a great beauty, yet, she radiated a definite charm. She was a most welcome sight as we were all thirsty.

Jeanine came again around noon to bring us a picnic lunch of baguettes, cold cuts, cheeses, fruits along with more wine and water. I opted for the water. At lunch, she stayed to talk to everyone and share our meal. She always exchanged a few words with me, asking about "l'Amérique", while offering glimpses into her life.

Over the next week, I learned more about Jeanine's life. She liked the harvest period because it gave her a chance to meet other young people. She got a break from piles of homework assigned by her all-girl Catholic school. Sunday was her favorite day. On that afternoon, Jeanine spent time in town to meet with friends in the café. They would go to a matinee at the local cinema. Her favorite singer was a French teen star named Johnny Holiday, a name I found oddly American. She thought he was cute, even more handsome than Elvis.

She would return again in mid-afternoon with drinks seeking each of us out as she walked up and down the rows.

With every new visit to the fields, Jeanine grew more alluring. By the middle of the second week, her plain country charm had evolved into an enchanting natural beauty. By the middle of the third week, I had begun to feel a part of the landscape, just another field hand while Jeanine had transformed into the princess of the vineyard. Her smiling face rose above the green bushes like a beacon of joy. When I learned that she collected stamps, a hobby my father avidly pursued, I offered to get her some from the United States. My father, being a generous man, sent her a big manila envelope filled with cancelled stamps. This gave rise to my only misunderstanding with Monsieur Morgeot.

Unfortunately for Jeanine, Monsieur Morgeot distrusted my exchanges with his daughter, or perhaps troubled by the indebtedness involved in accepting a gift from a stranger, returned the stamps to me. This did not distract from Jeanine's amazing transformation into a wood nymph which paralleled my own into a migrant field hand. The two of us continued to chat in the vineyards and daydream about the other's life, although we became more cautious in our exchanges after the incident.

At sunset each day, we workers returned to the farmhouse for bathing followed by another night of feasting and animated conversing. Bathing involved scrubbing down with a washcloth and a bar of soap over the sink. Drying off with a towel concluded the bath. One evening after washing, I lay face down in my shorts resting on the bed. One of the Italian field hands, Antonio, came over and kissed me, once on each calf muscle. It startled me, a gesture completely foreign to my puritan upbringing that, at first, evoked suspicions of homosexuality. Nevertheless, after living with the Italians for a few weeks, I understood when Antonio declared enthusiastically in a singsong French that mine were beautiful strong calves. He often made grand gestures to express his opinions when speaking passionately about the good food or when flattering the ladies. I realized that this act was another of his grand gestures. I began to feel a connection to this strange new world.

The days working in the field were long, although, not that physically demanding. The mental strain proved more exhausting. I felt frustrated by the lack of an outlet for my need to speak English or express more complex ideas during my three week stay. Still, an important benefit of this constant pressure to ask for everything, to explain everything in French, was that it forced me to search in my dictionary. My language skills began to improve. With each passing day, my French got a little better until, by the end of my stay at Gevrey Chambertin, I could manage to communicate all my basic needs and carry on a simple conversation in French.

Also, I absorbed new social behaviors. My sense of the inviolable space required between people was changing, distances growing smaller. Spontaneous outbursts of passion did not necessarily equate to anger. It became easier to touch others in a casual fashion without feeling I had abused their privacy. Best of all, I had discovered that these Europeans thought of me as a representative of "l'Amérique", a magical land that inspired their sense of wonder. For them, I was a special person. I was beginning to believe it myself.

Taking in the City
The farm at Gevrey Chambertin, a former medieval monastery, sat on a gentle knoll. Its large wooden gate opened onto a square courtyard enclosed on all four sides by moss covered stone walls. In one corner a tractor stuck out between two tall wooden doors while the flatbed trailer attached to it disappeared into the shadows of what looked like a cavernous barn. A few chickens hopped about the courtyard next to a small fenced vegetable garden. The

main farmhouse rose above the other buildings. Three stories high, it had a thick wooden door darkened by age and shuttered windows strategically placed a good two meters above the ground.

The lady in charge, Madame Morgeot, greeted me warmly. I followed her into the barn, then through double doors that led to a large dining hall and wine cellar. Just inside, a dark wooden table some fifteen feet in length paralleled the outer wall. Its thick top had long flat benches tucked under either side. Nicks and marks peppered its face, tell-tale scars suggesting many years of feasting and reveling had passed over its surface.

At the far end, we climbed a staircase leading to a dormitory. Eight beds were lined up in a row, each one separated by a small night stand. A thin mattress lay on the pine platform of each bed covered by a sheet, a straw pillow and one woolen blanket. The only sink in the room stood against the back wall. Next to it, a narrow door led to a small toilette. This toilette consisted of a hole in the floor with two raised islands on either side to stand and squat. A white porcelain knob hung at the end of a rusty chain suspended from the ceramic bowl mounted high above. A roll of brown paper dangled over a wire loop nailed to the adjacent wall. The rough character of this place put me at ease. Jack Karouac would have undoubtedly approved.

My timing was great. I had arrived just as preparations for the evening meal were in progress. Soon the dinner bell rang and the workers began to arrive. They were an eclectic mix of young people from Spain and Italy. The group also included another French student from Dijon. This gathering was largely made up of males However, a female French student and a Spanish girl counted among them. None of the workers spoke in English.

Everyone crowded onto the benches, passing bread around the table. Madame Morgeot and her daughter, Jeanine, a girl a few years younger than myself, poured wine from clay pitchers which they periodically refilled at the oak barrels behind us. It is amazing how quickly the mind learns basic language skills when the belly is growling. I was soon calling out in French to pass the bread, to fill my plate with more meat, potatoes and vegetables, and of course, to fill my glass.

Beer had been my drink of choice in Australia. Here, I discovered the wonderful wine of Gevrey Chambertin. People in this country did not drink in the manner of the Australians. Wine was a part of their daily life, a fundamental component of the main meals. These people showed no interest in getting drunk for recreational pleasure, nor did they seem to need alcohol to inspire their imaginations or ignite their passions.

As the meal progressed, a chorus of voices filled the room building to an explosion of gaiety and laughter. Everyone was talking at the same time, but no one seemed to mind. The Italians around me formed a mini-convention focusing in on me. They used markedly slow speech for my benefit, pointing out utensils, foods, and dishes. It became a game of sorts. They nurtured me with words to pronounce and laughed in satisfaction at my modest successes. I felt like a puppy getting a treat every time I rolled over or shook hands. My treats were delicious plates of food, fresh baked bread, and wine served up in an atmosphere of merriment.

The evening carried on like this until the flow of words slowed to a trickle, overpowered by drooping eyelids and warm bellies. After all, everyone but me had just labored ten hours in the fields. We, eight males, climbed the back stairs to our rigid beds while the ladies disappeared into another part of the house.

Just before sunrise, the roosters helped us out of our beds along with Monsieur Morgeot who turned on the lights. After a quick breakfast of bread and butter washed down with a bowl of warm café au lait, we climbed on the flat-bed trailer, rubber boots dangling over the edge, and headed out for the vineyards. A short ride away, long rows of grapes awaited us in the cool dampness of a thin light at daybreak.

We carried wooden baskets with wire handles. At first, my hands were cold and the constant stooping and bending to pluck grapes made my back hurt. Finally, I adapted to the chill. A bit hungry, but mostly curious, I ate a few grapes. They were bitter-sweet and full of seeds, not all that tasty. As the sun slowly rose to warm my body, I settled into a rhythm moving gradually down the rows.

At mid morning, Jeanine came up the dirt path dressed in a modest cotton smock and tall rubber boots. She carried a bucket filled with water and a large jug of wine. Jeanine did not strike me as a great beauty, yet, she radiated a definite charm. She was a most welcome sight as we were all thirsty. Jeanine came again around noon to bring us a picnic lunch of baguettes, cold cuts, cheeses, fruits along with more wine and water. I chose the water. At lunch, she stayed to talk to everyone and share our meal. She always exchanged a few words with me, asking about "l'Amérique", while offering glimpses into her life in simple French.

Over the next week, I managed to decipher pieces of Jeanine's life. She liked the harvest period because it gave her a chance to meet other young people. She got a break from piles of homework assigned by her all-girl Catholic school. Sunday was her favorite day. On that afternoon, Jeanine spent time in town to meet with friends in the café and go to a matinee at the local cinema. Her favorite singer was a French teen star named Johnny Hallyday, a name I

85

found oddly American. She thought he was cute, even more handsome than Elvis.

She would return again in mid-afternoon with drinks seeking each of us out as she walked up and down the rows. With every new visit to the fields, Jeanine grew more alluring. By the middle of the second week, her plain country charm had evolved into an enchanting natural beauty. By the middle of the third week, I had begun to feel a part of the landscape, just another field hand, while Jeanine had transformed into the princess of the vineyard. Her smiling face rose above the green bushes like a beacon of joy.

At sunset each evening, we returned to the farmhouse for bathing followed by another night of feasting and animated conversing. Bathing involved scrubbing down with a washcloth and a bar of soap over the sink. Drying off with a towel concluded the bath. One evening after washing, I lay face down in my briefs resting on the bed. Antonio, one of the Italian field hands, came over and kissed me, once on each calf muscle. It startled me. This gesture, which was so completely foreign to my puritan upbringing that it led me to wonder if he was gay. But, having already spent a few weeks with the Italians, I quickly recognized his swagger when Antonio declared enthusiastically in a singsong French that I had strong calves. He often made bold gestures and spoke passionately to express himself about food or when flattering the ladies. I realized that this act was another of his grand gestures. I began to feel a connection to this strange new world.

The days working in the field were long, although, not that physically demanding. The mental strain of not being able to express myself proved more exhausting. I felt frustrated by my lack of ability to express more complex ideas during my three week stay. Still, an important benefit of this constant pressure to ask for everything, to explain everything in French, was that it forced me to return often to my dictionary. My language skills began to improve. With each passing day, my French got a little better until, by the end of my stay at Gevrey Chambertin, I could manage to communicate all my basic needs and carry on a simple conversation in French.

Also, I absorbed new social behaviors. My sense of the inviolable space required between people was changing, distances growing smaller. Spontaneous outbursts of passion did not necessarily equate to anger. It became easier to touch others in a casual fashion without feeling I had abused their privacy. Best of all, I had discovered that these Europeans thought of me as a representative of "l'Amérique", someone mysterious from a magical land that inspired their sense of wonder. For them, I was a special person. I was beginning to believe it myself.

Taking in the City

Upon my return to Dijon, the walking began. Classes did not start for another week. It was October and I had enough money to pay bills through the end of the year. The two mile hike downtown became a daily routine as I loved walking through the streets watching people go about their lives. Walking filled the same need to process my experiences as those long evenings spent at the bow of the cargo ships. I had no idea who I was in this land, only who I was not. So observing from the fringe of society evolved into a cultural initiation. Watching the behavior of the locals, I attempted to imitate their mannerisms and adapt their behaviors.

I started my walks at the student residences, surrounded by empty farmland at the edge of the city. Walking to the town center, I noticed that the newer homes on the outskirts gradually vanished, replaced by older neighborhoods with narrower streets. Both old and new buildings were constructed as if the citizenry anticipated a war. Heavy metal shutters could completely block off the windows of the concrete and stone buildings. Thick doors sealed entrances. Even the restaurants and shops could be converted into impenetrable fortresses at nightfall.

Older adults and young people mixed comfortably as if age were not very important. I often saw grown women walking arm in arm or holding hands. When groups of people met, the men always shook hands with the other men and kissed all the women twice, once on each cheek. This was a practice I had learned at Gevrey Chambertin. At first, kissing the girls stirred up mild sensual undercurrents. With time, it felt very natural. I began to love this way of greeting as it made the women seem like sisters and the men like long time friends. Yet, when strangers encountered one another, there was always that probing stare. It was not possible for me to be invisible. People in the streets would peer at me intensely with a blank expression.

Not really hostile, but completely uninhibited about staring so intently. I got used to the unwavering attention. I realized they were studying me from head to toe and began to gaze back with equal curiosity, to study them. I noticed they watched each other in the same way as if engaged in some kind of national pastime. Being seen in public took on a whole new meaning.

Many restaurants and cafés were arranged to indulge this pastime. Some had tables and chairs set up just outside on terraces under umbrellas, others set up seating on enclosed patios along the street. People settled into the cafes at midday or in the evening. Many talked out of the sides of their mouths, only half listening, all the while wide-eyed, surveying the passers-by. Others locked eyes, engaged in animated dialog that made me wonder what crucial topic inspired these ardent conversations.

During this time, I was beginning to speculate about my prospects in this perplexing land. I was going to be a college student an important representative of "l'Amérique" and in that first week, no other foreigners crossed my path as I walked around Dijon.

Leaves began to fall from the trees as my one cotton sweater no longer kept me warm. A new tempo evolved in my stride. My pace slowed while walking in the sunny patches only to pick up considerably when I passed into the shady parts of the road. To help compensate for the biting chill, I began to stop and buy a bar of chocolate at a patisserie on my way to town. In the shaded sections, I would take a bite. Letting the piece melt in my mouth, I concentrated on the rich sweet flavor rather than the cold air. I could not afford a new coat. In contrast to the cost of room and board, clothing was much more expensive here than in the United States. It was time to swallow my pride and fall back on my support system. I wrote home asking for a package of warmer clothing from my bedroom closet in California. I had reason to believe that my parents wouldn't mind this request.

Correspondence with my parents over the past year had been sporadic. Nevertheless, I wrote home once every few months. I had never asked for anything since leaving the States. Throughout my youth, Dad often warned me I would have to pay my own way once I turned eighteen. My father was one of ten children who grew up on a farm in Colebrook, Ohio. His father had died at the young age of forty-seven leaving my grandmother and all those children to fend for themselves during the Great Depression.

Being the second oldest son, the task of keeping the family together fell to him and my uncle. My father's life had been a struggle to prevail. He met the challenge. Rising out of poverty through hard work, he became an accomplished physicist and from the time I was young, he expected both my brother and me to hold our own in the world. So, the letter I sent him just before leaving for the grape harvest evoked an unexpected response.

After paying my tuition, meal ticket, room and board a month in advance, I had almost no cash left. I had written my parents a letter which I mailed the day of my departure to the grape harvest. It included a comment advising them not to worry if they did not hear from me for awhile. I explained that I could not afford the additional cost of stamps since the last of my money had gone to pay for the bus ticket to Gevrey Chambertin. Upon my return from "les vendanges", the director of the foreign studies program approached me demanding that I write my father at once. My father had contacted the University inquiring after my welfare. He wanted to know whether or not it would be necessary for him to fly to France to "take the matter in hand".

I explained to the director that I had received some pay shortly after my arrival at Gevrey Chambertin. That I had already written home and told my parents how my situation had improved. However, it surprised me to discover the extent of my father's concern. It seemed likely that in their current state of mind, my parents would send my old clothing. Shortly, mom mailed a letter announcing the clothes were on the way. Dad added a note scribbled on scratch paper which addressed my acceptance to French university. It read simply, "You have achieved something noteworthy." From that time on, my feelings towards my parents began to improve.

The Foreign Studies Program
In late fall, new faces started appearing all around town. The dorms filled with young people as did the cafés. The streets bustled with life while lines at the student restaurant grew longer and noisier. A modern school cafeteria had opened conveniently located close to the dorms and designed for functionality. The steel and glass structure of the new cafeteria furnished with plastic chairs and Formica ta-

bles on linoleum floors reminded me of my high school lunchroom.

I preferred going into town to eat at the old restaurant. It was located on the second floor of one of the ivy covered stone buildings in the center of the city. The tables and chairs were made of hardwood. As the room filled with student voices and plates clattered against trays, the sounds of youth floated across the open refectory with a resonance that echoed high overhead across the lofty ceiling. Once inside, a magnificent sky filled the large room through a wide expanse of leaded glass windows that covered the full height of the fifteen foot outer wall. Occasional bursts of light sprayed across the oak floor, splashing against the back wall. On sunny days, the hall glistened like a waiting room at the gates of heaven.

On the last Wednesday in October, the Foreign Student Program held its Fall orientation. The new students met in a classroom near the old cafeteria. About twenty-five students were gathered comfortably in the room waiting in small groups for the meeting to begin. The department chair, wearing a grey suit, sat behind a desk reviewing paperwork.

Much to my surprise, English was being spoken at one corner of the room where some half dozen young people had congregated. The young men wore mohair or dark wool trench coats; some had on white shirts and ties. They looked Ivy League, like big city rich kids. Two oddly mismatched girls standing together in another corner caught my attention. One had a well-healed appearance.

She wore a red, black, and white coordinated outfit which could still have had the sales tag hanging from it somewhere. Her smooth skin was big and round, stretched tight as a balloon. Her remote comportment and tense-lipped demeanor gave the impression of one of those Russian

91

nesting dolls. At her side stood a petite, willowy creature dressed in denim jeans and a modest cotton sweater. Long straight black hair followed the contour her shoulders framing an olive-skinned face with penetrating dark eyes.

She looked mature for a young person, almost ageless, vaguely resembling those opaque female faces I had seen in Italian Renaissance paintings in art books. If it were not for her New York City accent, she could have passed as French.

In another corner, stood a group that, at first, I took to be Americans because of their fair skin and brightly colored clothing. I realized my mistake when they began speaking an unknown language with a modulated pitch that had a melodic, bouncing ball, inflection. The way they spoke sounded friendly and inviting. I began to suspect they were from one of the Nordic countries. Continuing to scan the room, the remaining small groups interested me less, obviously these youth had not ventured far from home by coming to France. Most likely they were from Spain or Italy. They seemed to be fluent in French.

We took seats when the professor began to speak. He went over the program details. He was speaking in French which required all my attention to understand. With an authoritative stance, this elderly gentleman scratched out a daunting schedule in white chalk on a blackboard. We were to have one class of 'linguistics', three classes of French literature and one class of French history. The program consisted of twelve hours of classes per week with final exams to be held at the end of the scholastic year spread over a two week period. All but the linguistics classes were a part of the regular liberal arts curriculum for French students. I barely knew how to speak French, struggled to read the newspaper. Yet, somehow fate had led me this far, and the university program represented something "noteworthy" to attempt. In the process, room and board would be dirt cheap and there were lots of interesting characters to get to know better.

Going back to speaking English all the time held little appeal, but taking a break from continually using only French proved too great a temptation to resist. I joined the group of Americans after orientation to get acquainted. There were only eight of us. The loudest talkers were some city slickers from Chicago. Jack, the big baritone, acted like he knew all about France. With a sleek haircut and clean shaven, he presented well in that mohair ensemble. Everything matched right down to his brown penny loafers and patterned brown socks. Roger, who dressed slightly more modestly, served as his cheer leader reverently agreeing with every word that came out of Jack's mouth. They seemed to be looking around for an errand boy to carry their bags.

Their dress looked sharp in an American way. Still, by this time I had become sufficiently aware to know that the loose cut of their clothes contrasted with the latest in French fashion. A small detail to be sure, but it clashed with the way they boasted of having mastered the French lifestyle. Did they even speak French? I wondered. From the beginning, it seemed unlikely that they would admit their ignorance. Like kids living inside a plastic bubble, I suspected that they were going to bounce around Dijon without ever touching the place.

We walked over to the Café du Nord on the Place Darcy to get acquainted. The group spread out as we settled into chrome chairs around several small tables. I sat near the two American girls, maneuvering away from Jack and Roger.

Jean, the Russian nesting doll, spoke first. "Sue and I just came from Paris; I found a place in Dijon on the boulevard, near classes. God knows what could happen around here at night." She said in a tense voice. Jean appeared uncomfortable, her eyes searching for reassurance.

I responded, "The French seem nice. Like a kind sort of people, even though they don't act friendly at first. I feel better in this place than I did in Hamburg."
"They seem ok to me," Susan, the willowy one, chimed in as she quietly surveyed the plaza. Her voice was calm, analytical. As she looked out intently over the passing crowd, her eyes took on an impenetrable quality.
"You sound like New Yorkers. What you doin' here?" I asked.

Sue abruptly redirected her attention. Her voice took on a fierce intensity as she turned and looked me straight in the eye. "I'm here to learn French," she insisted. Her eyes locked onto mine like radar commanding undivided attention. "My father says I'm wasting time here. He wouldn't give me a dime toward the trip to Israel last year. I had to work... a full year, just to save up the money. He doesn't approve of France either. Thinks it's another waste of time; thinks I should be in school in New York. I was planning on coming by myself to Paris. Jean, here, tagged along. We met on that Zionist trip to Israel. I switched to Dijon; it's cheaper to live here."

The determination in her voice gave a sense of how hard she must have struggled to get here. Those dark eyes now filled with defiance. I understood Sue. She was pursuing her dream with the ferocity of a mountain lion stalking a deer. I knew her obstinacy. I recognized her resoluteness to triumph over the attitude of her father. Her father surpassed mine in severity, but they seemed to share a common bullheadedness.

Sue currently lived with a French family. She told me about the husband's attempts to get in the bathroom while she was taking a bath. He claimed she was using too much water. She didn't trust him and had locked the door. She was looking around for a new place to live with a French student. There could be no doubt that this girl was going to learn French.

Jean sat in silence. She ignored me and Sue, looking to participate in the larger group of Americans.
A few tables away, Jack had cranked up the volume hoping to extend his realm of influence. I shifted further in my chair. With my back to them, I began to tell Sue about my experiences. She followed my adventures with that same directed focus of attention. We hit it off right away. I felt we were going to become friends on a common mission to explore this new land and share our discoveries.

That night, after a mediocre dinner at the student restaurant and a chilly walk across town, I settled into my warm room in the student dorms. I planned to look into getting some of the school books the next day. This left the evening for me to relax and work on some melodies I was trying to master.

A complete lack of musical talent did not stop me from practicing on my plastic recorder. It was a cheap, cream-colored instrument that I had picked up in Aden. The recorder could well have been out of tune and I would have never noticed the difference. I had managed to construct the first few bars of "Green Sleeves" and "Stranger on the Shore" from memory. I began to toot away sitting on my bed trying to refine and expand the sounds, hoping that a few more bars might miraculously escape through the noise.

Suddenly, a pounding rattled my door and a Frenchman's voice growled from the other side, "Qu'est-ce passe là-dedans."(What's going on in there?)

95

Much to my surprise, when I opened the door, there stood a young Frenchman almost as tall as me. I tensed up a bit expecting my first brush with trouble on French soil. The young man stood back as if he were in shock. As his eyes moved up and down, sizing me up in that uniquely French way, his attitude began to change. What appeared at first to be an angry expression and tense stance relaxed with the movement of his probing gaze.

"Qu'est que je peux faire pour vous?"(How can I help you ?) I asked in my Yankee accent. As I spoke, a large warm smile came across his face. He extended his hand stepping into my room with such ease that I thought maybe I was being welcomed into his room.

He switched to English. "Do you speak English? So sorry to disturb you, but I couldn't help wondering where that lovely music was coming from. You play so well!" Are you a music student?" he asked. Then came the question I was by now expecting. "Are you from America?" His face coalesced into one big Cheshire cat smile. This wasn't my room anymore; it was Wonderland. Ah yes, "l'Amérique" to the rescue.
"I'm from the United States" I replied in English shaking his hand warmly.

"Excellent, excellent, I am most pleased to meet you! Let me present myself. I am your neighbor, Felix. I am a student at the business school here. It would seem from your accent that you are already learning French. What an interesting country America is! Where do you come from in America and why did you choose Dijon of all places?" he said in a most engaging way.

This fellow was a pleasant surprise. He seemed very interested in Americans and clearly wanted to practice his English. Even though I preferred to speak French, he was the friendliest Frenchman I had met so far. I put my recorder away for the night. Inviting him to stay for a while, I offered him a cup of my cheap instant coffee which I suspected he would say tasted great.

He was from a small town outside of Lyon called Cours. It was surprising that he spoke English so well with only a moderate accent. As my new friend described his small town with its history of textile mills and green hills, his eyes sparkled with pride and his voice filled with enthusiasm. He even seemed to think I would love the local goat cheese. He recommended the region's grilled frog's legs cooked as only the chefs in his pays (home town) could prepare them. He was making me hungry. It was looking like the beginning of a fruitful friendship.

High Expectations
The Foreign Student Program only vaguely resembled an official university curriculum. It was as if a handful of students suddenly appeared one day and the school had to figure out what to do with them. The only class dedicated to us foreigners was *linguistics*. This was a basic grammar course where we learned to conjugate French verbs and other essential language skills.

We could pick any literature and history courses we wanted to attend. Barely able to follow what the teachers were saying, I sat in on several of the classes considering my options. Eventually, I discovered that the contemporary novels were easier to read than the classics. Some of the more contemporary writers like André Malraux wrote using a more accessible French. Other poets like Rimbaud and Baudelaire were presented as rebellious, raising my level of motivation to understand what they were writing.

The first novel that I attempted to read was *l'Etranger*. Just the title, *The Stranger* (which can also be translated as

The Foreigner) was enough to get me interested. It was about a young man who behaved with indifference to his own fate, with an odd detachment from the world. I instantly felt a connection with this attitude. The author, Albert Camus turned out to have been born and raised in one of the French colonies, Algeria. At the time, Algeria had just won its independence from France. Camus had moved to France as an adult and must have faced the challenges of any outsider trying to fit into this unique culture.

My favorite professor was Pierre Gallon, the teacher of French drama. He was a tall gangly man with thick feminine lips, a big head and a bigger voice. His classes were held in a large semicircular amphitheater that seated a hundred people. In the late fifties, Professor Gallon had been a member of France's most prestigious theater troop, *La Comedie Francaise.* This famous troop had been in existence for several hundred years in Paris and had performed for French kings. Professor Gallon's voice filled the amphitheater as he bellowed out passages from Moliere giving life to the characters. Even though I only understood a handful of words, Professor Gallon's jests, expressions, and intonations brought each character to life.

French history classes were the most overwhelming. There seemed to be so many people and events throughout French history. All the people had complicated titles and even more complicated relationships, as power constantly changed hands and new alliances were formed. I couldn't keep track of all these facts. I doubt that I would have been able to follow this history even in English.

As I struggled to make progress through the onslaught of information, I eventually focused on two important considerations. The first was that there would be no possible way for me to absorb enough of the material to graduate in nine months. The second discovery came as I began to understand the French university system. Just about anyone could get into a French university, even me. The rigorous final exams offset the relaxed enrollment requirements.

Only about one in ten people actually passed the exams. To compensate for this dismal success rate, students were allowed to try again if they had failed. They were permitted to re-enroll each year until they either passed the class or gave up. All the while, the generous subsidies to students miraculously continued.

I came up with a workable approach. For the literature and theater classes, I would start out reading the material written by authors who wrote in a more accessible French. For the history classes, I purchased an old set of the French history texts, the kind used to teach high school students. Lastly, I would attend all the grammar classes since those were truly oriented toward students learning the French language.

That first month of school, I attended classes and read forty hours a week. I spent many an hour in the student library with a novel and a dictionary plugging away. I made progress on both my knowledge of the French language and my cultural education. Meanwhile, my social life was minimal. I wasn't speaking much French and grew tired of living between the pages of books. I decided this was no fun and began to spend more time in the cafes.

By now, Jack and Roger had managed to create a small following. They lived in the next dorm over from mine. Their crowd was made up of a handful of English and Americans who preferred creating a mini-colonial world to getting involved with the French. I still hung out with them on occasion for a break and to speak some English.
One cold night in late November, we congregated in Jack's room. He had purchased a big fried chicken for the group.

Spouting some phony philosophy about manliness and getting in touch with the primitive beast inside, he encouraged the group to rip the chicken apart with their bare hands and devour the bird right down to the bone. They ripped away munching tendons and skin until only a small pile of clean bones remained. Jack declared that they had proven themselves to be true men. I did not participate. To me, it seemed sad that they wouldn't apply that same enthusiasm to participating in French student life.

This was the night Jack hinted at how he had acquired his large and seemingly expensive wardrobe. He had been a manager of an exclusive men's clothing store in Chicago. A job he got through his family's political connections. He claimed to be from a wealthy family, one of his more believable assertions.

Occasionally, when a big shipment arrived at the store, he would work late into the night. He stayed until long after all the employees had gone home. Jack said, "It was extra work that merited extra rewards." We all knew what "extra rewards" he was referring to with his sly smile.
I didn't care too much if Jack had ripped off the fancy store or that he bragged so much about his cleverness. What did bother me was his complete lack of effort to connect with France or speak French.

However, I did understand one of his problems, one we all faced. It was especially hard to make friends with French students given our limited ability to speak the language Most of the French students spoke very little English. They had all studied it in high school, but rarely had occasion to actually carry on a conversation. In addition, it was hard to join their tightly knit groups. They seemed to have known each other since childhood and showed little interest in foreigners.

For a short time, I made an effort to develop a relationship with a French girl named Francoise. She spoke almost no English. Hoping to make her my girlfriend, I struggled to talk about the weather, the buses, the restaurants, anything. I tried to make conversation using words I had picked up at the grape harvest or remembered from the dictionary. These were patchwork conversations with little emotional substance. Things got awkward quickly. Francoise stared at me with a blank expression; her smile seemed strained during the long silences. At least she did smile. I could tell she also wanted to communicate with me. Eventually, Francoise rejoined friends from her village. Once again at ease, she talked freely with them, demonstrating her warm affectionate qualities. I knew that I needed a new approach to improve my conversational French.

When I started hanging around the student cafes, a new opportunity emerged. Instead of sitting with the Americans, I joined the tables where those foreign students in the brightly colored clothes were sitting. They were open and curious, welcoming me into their circle. We shared a common goal to improve our ability to speak French. They still broke off to speak in their native language from time to time but, at least it wasn't English. We spoke slowly to each other piecing together messages with the few hundred French words each had mastered. It worked. I was able to learn that they were mostly from Norway through some exchange program set up by the universities in both countries. They were all a few years older than me.

These Scandinavians displayed an optimistic attitude toward the French, the food, the coffee in the cafes, and me. The girls dressed in bright green and yellow ensembles with matching colored ribbons in their hair. They looked like dolls. This was not really in fashion in France at the time. Yet, all three of the Norwegian girls were stunning beauties. Checking them over closely, I could definitely imagine myself chasing them around the tables, ribbons sailing in the air.

The group always invited me to join them, but in short order, the girls returned to speaking Norwegian. Unfortunately, their interest lay elsewhere as they settled into their chairs while eyeing the Frenchmen passing by. They delighted in those dark eyed mystery men crisscrossing sidewalks in front of us. I never got as much as a smile. For them, I must have looked too familiar, just another blue eyed youngster.

I spent most of the time talking to Jan. A token male acquaintance as far as the girls were concerned, Jan was more of a mascot and faired no better than me with the northern enchantresses. After all, he was a blond haired Norwegian. Jan clearly knew more about those girls than I did because he didn't mind being ignored. He was easy going with a positive outlook. We enjoyed talking about the classes and our discoveries while wandering around town. He lived in my building and we became casual friends. Jan had a bicycle. It was getting colder every day now as winter approached. My clothes had not yet arrived from California and biking to town on a cold day was better than the long walk. After borrowing Jan's bike a few times, I began to look around to buy a used one. I soon found an old beat up clunker for next to nothing.

One evening, much to my amazement, we were all invited to a reception by the Mayor of Dijon. At this reception, it became clear that many of these young people were not typical students. The Mayor of Dijon hosted the reception for the foreign students in the old refectory downtown. It was a quite formal reception. Waiters in uniforms wearing white gloves walked about the room carrying silver trays of snacks and Champaign. They looked very ceremonious.

The Mayor made a welcoming speech pausing to acknowledge each of the children of diplomats from the various countries they represented. The students were sons and daughters of officials from South America, Italy, and Vietnam, as well as some Scandinavian countries. Even though the embassies were in Paris, the young people had come to Dijon. As it turned out, most of the members of our small group of foreign students were either the children of diplomats or came from wealthy, big city families. Even Jean seemed to have plenty of money. The only exceptions I knew of at the time were me and Susan. Sue did not show up at the reception.

Colette
Sue rarely hung out with the other foreign students. Her fiercely independent nature combined with a tenacious approach to mastering all the course material led her to live in a state of self imposed isolation. The few times I did find Sue in a cafe she was reading some French book. Just to get her to look up from her reading was a challenge. I had to raise my voice or make a loud noise before she would put the book down. The effort had its rewards.

When Sue finally did notice me, I was always welcomed with a compassionate smile. "Hi, Richie" came her big hearted greeting, followed by her undivided attention. She called me *Richie* from the day she learned my name was Richard. *Richie!* Of all the nicknames, I would have never picked a little kid's nickname like that. Normally, it would have made me angry. Yet, Sue said it with such affection that I felt really special. Reducing the physical distance between us when she talked to me created a feeling of genuine intimacy. Her sense of personal space was much like that of the French.
"How ya doin' Richie? Are you alright?" Sue would say searching with those warm brown eyes to detect my feelings. Here was a girl who seemed wholeheartedly interest-

103

ed in my life. Having spent my youth almost exclusively in the company of other males, I didn't know that it was possible to be friends with a girl. I liked this new friendship. We often talked about our travels. She enjoyed hearing my adventures in Australia while her descriptions of Israel made the country sound so beautiful and fascinating. Israel had places called kibbutzim where people could live and eat in exchange for work in the fields. Some communal farms even held "Ulpans," schools where young people could stay and learn Hebrew half of the day if they worked in the fields the other half.

Sue eventually managed to break away from Jean and locate a small flat. The place was a modest two rooms on the second floor of an ancient stone building. It was not far from the center on a major boulevard called "Rue de la Liberté". The first room consisted of a twin bed near the window with a small kitchen by the front door. A tiny wooden table and two plain straight back chairs were crowded into a nook next to the stove. The second room, a cramped bedroom, had a sink in one corner and a twin bed in the other. Heavy hinged shutters hung outside the tall windows of each room with a view to the boulevard below.

Thick pieces of old paint just below the surface gave a lumpy effect to the recently painted radiators. Sue found a French student to move in and share the expenses. The rent must have been cheap.

Unlike the other Americans, Sue and I spoke French with each other most of the time. Since her knowledge of French was about the same level as mine, we were able to help each other learn the language. I started making regular visits to Sue's flat on the days I wandered around downtown.
Her new roommate, Colette, came from Auvergne, a region in the south central part of France. The daughter of a

gas station owner, she was studying political science and only spoke with us in French.

Colette dressed simply. She often wore baggy jeans and ribbed sweaters with buttons along one shoulder, the kind frequently worn by French factory workers. Colette's skin was that olive shade of the Mediterranean peoples. She had short curly hair and wore heavy brown work shoes. Her rugged, slightly weathered, look reminded me of some of the young people with whom I had worked during the grape harvest.

Colette had a strong, well toned body, her nice figure discernible in spite of the loosely fitting jeans and sweaters. She possessed a self-assured quiet, beauty cloaked behind the outward appearance of ordinariness. There was an attractive quality to her self-confident temperament. She exuded a remarkable intensity of concentration when she spoke, that same intensity I had first noticed in Sue. They were well-suited to be roommates.

Colette dreamed on a grand scale. She focused on the politics of social change and revolution. She belonged to a small, but radical, student group of Trotskyites, an extreme wing that had broken with the Communist party. They committed themselves to converting France into a radical Socialist society. Her passionate monologs on the need for reform in France began to captivate Sue.

For my part, I mostly liked hearing the French language, occasionally stopping her to ask the meaning of words. Her ideas on the redistribution of wealth only mildly interested me. I eventually concluded that I could only be a recipient of such a scheme. Unfortunately, Colette didn't appear to have much wealth to distribute. It vaguely occurred to me that her group might provide me with some badly needed warmer clothing. Even that didn't seem likely.

105

The most enjoyable aspect of our conversations came down to the three of us sharing an evening over a baguette, some Camembert and a bottle of Burgundy. On other occasions, we speculated in the late morning over bowls of café au lait and croissants.

None of the other members of Colette's group ever visited the flat when I was there. Although, I did hear of their activities. She told us about their midnight runs through the streets of Dijon to tear down posters the Communist Student League had illegally put up around town. Her team would then replace them with Trotsky posters. Her ideas regarding the importance of these clandestine missions made little sense to me. Unschooled in political strategy, I couldn't see the point in sticking up more dull colorless posters. Nevertheless, both Sue and I were invited to come along and watch for police patrols.

Sue seemed to be getting progressively more interested in Colette's ideas of social change. The need for a more compassionate treatment of the disadvantaged was clearly deeply influencing her. Sue really seemed fascinated by the Trotsky philosophy, but did not want to go on these night missions for fear of getting kicked out of France. The night runs sounded like they might make for a daring adventure to me. On the other hand, it had been drummed into my head from childhood that the Communists were bad guys who wanted to drop atom bombs on the U.S. I couldn't see the point in helping her group since they, too, probably wanted to bomb Elm Grove Elementary.

Re-runs flashed through my mind of years of childhood training in that small Tennessee schoolhouse. We all knew the drill. A screeching siren would sound in the middle of class and we would all dive under our little wooden desks, hoping our bottoms weren't sticking out too far.
One night after, a particularly lively cheese and wine fest, Colette retired to her room, leaving the door open. Was she

waiting for me to follow her in? Then she made an unexpected offer.

It astonished me so much that I turned to Sue and said in English, "Do you know what she just asked me?"
"What?"
"She just asked me if I wanted to sleep with her. What do you think?" I bumbled astounded, lacking the nerve to answer Colette directly.

Sue looked calmly at me, pausing for what seemed like an eternity, then coolly replied, "Sure, why not?"

This was a new experience that did not fit any of my imagined guidelines about courtship, love or sex. Weren't we supposed to be in love or at least be affectionate with some level of intimacy? If not, wasn't I supposed to pay?
There was no way I could turn down such a wonderful offer. Sex with no obligations! Especially since another female encouraged me to accept the offer. If this freedom of behavior was part of communist philosophy, I was ready to make my contribution to the cause, at least until the morning.

Colette and I had a good time that night even though neither of us was very accomplished in the subtler skills of lovemaking. We undressed without embarrassment. For the first time, I felt entirely comfortable being so intimate with a woman; this woman who seemed willing to share equally in the giving and receiving of pleasure. Ours was a "from each according to their abilities and to each according to their needs" kind of lovemaking, with the emphasis on the "needs". Afterwards, we snuggled close, our naked bodies molded together in the small bed and fell asleep. The next morning, we woke up in good spirits, still friends.

The Deal

Back at the dorms, my new French buddy, Félix, and I got along famously. At first, he wanted to speak only English, but with time became more willing to speak French with me. He didn't hesitate to correct my many errors and taught me new phrases. He even invited me to spend Christmas break with his family in Cours.

I learned important words like "merde," which is loosely translated as "shit" in English. However, this is one of the most versatile expressions in the French language. This word could convey many feelings such as anger, excitement, curiosity, or surprise. It came in handy to vent disappointment with a situation and was generally well received among students. Its use also separated the bold and free-spirited from the prudish who resorted to the watered down, "zut, alors" an alternative that lacked the same impact, but was more acceptable in polite society.

As the season progressed, nightfall came earlier and the air got colder. We found ourselves more frequently confined to the university housing by bad weather. One cold evening after dinner with nothing interesting to do, Félix and I walked over to Jack's room to see what was happening. Roger was already there sitting on the bed. Carl hung back, leaning against the radiator by the window. Félix didn't hesitate to open the conversation. He whirled around the tiny room shaking each person's hand, greeting them warmly. Presenting himself as a student of business, he professed great admiration for the mighty American economy and spirit of free enterprise.

Jack seized the opportunity, "Roger and I come from the great city of Chicago in the heart of *America* where some of the most important business transactions take place. In fact, we're the nation's commercial hub with a skyline higher than New York City's. We have the mighty Sears Tower, the tallest building in *America*." Jack kept emphasizing that word "America". By this time, he had picked up on the French fascination with "l'Amérique".

"Ahh *tchikago*!!" Félix chimed in, "A great city, the greatest! All Frenchmen know about this great city. We all see the movies. Al Capone, a really tough one, aye! And of course not to forget the *beefstek, merveilleux!* The biggest and thickest steaks. You are truly a lucky fellow!" Félix stepped closer and put his arm around Jack's shoulder giving him a warm hug.

Jack quickly pulled away looking a little startled. Securing more space between them, he continued, "Roger and I attend the University of Illinois which has the best business school in all of "America" he proclaimed, watching out of the corner of his eye for Félix's reaction.

"And what must you think of our modest little town of Dijon? You surely find it quite dull, oui?" Félix smiled humbly, inviting Jack to get himself more deeply snarled in the sticky web of his own vanity.

Jack forged ahead with his testimonial, oblivious to the implications of Félix's question. "It's ok, definitely not like Paris. We would be in Paris if not for our business school making special arrangements with the school here."

"It's starting to get damned cold here. We really need a car to get around town comfortably. Don't you think?" Jack fished around with his question. It sounded to me like he was brewing up some dubious plan in that calculating mind of his.

"Ah, this is only the beginning my friend. It is going to become very much colder! We are not far from the Swiss Alps. It's the snow, my dear friend, the snow is coming! And the wind, oh *mon dieux*, the wind!

" Félix's expression becoming serious, his voice deepened. Silence settled over the crowded little room as all eyes turned to Félix who furrowed his brow, consumed in thought. He rocked his head back and forth on his shoulders as if shaking around thoughts in his brain that were about to converge into a plan and work their way out of his mouth.

Then, suddenly, Félix's face lit up and that irresistible smile returned. He spoke in a pensive voice carefully pacing his speech, "I know a mechanic who works in a garage here. If you want, I can talk to him and get you a special deal on an eight-month lease of one of his cars. He's a good type and will take pity on us poor students. If you really want to avoid the cold morning trip to class… hmmm, we'll see what can be done." Félix's voice trailed off, as if waiting for images of cold morning trips to be conjured up in the room.

After a long pause, Jack took the lead, "Well, Félix, it would have to be an exceptionally good deal for me to put any money into this car. It would be nice to have a car when winter hits, I have to admit." He paused for a moment, most likely remembering those cold Chicago winters and the icy winds that whip across Lake Michigan.

"We would have to share the expenses," Jack waved his hand loosely around the room in the direction of the other Americans. "We would pay half and you, Félix, would have to pay the other half." Jack was hatching his version of the deal including the other Americans in a scheme that most likely didn't involve him paying much of anything. Jack delivered his proposal in a cool, somewhat challenging tone while holding his body stiff as if ready to strike. Félix seemed completely relaxed, self assured. From what I knew of him, Félix was being unusually friendly and had turned up the charm a notch. He almost always spoke in a loud voice, but had toned it down a tad, giving the impression of greater sincerity.

I quickly jumped in to let my situation be known, "Count me out; I'm almost out of money. It's going to be walking in the snow for me with the occasional bus ride in the worst weather." It was more than my lack of cash that stopped me. I sensed a game of wits was going on. A shady deal was brewing in which I wanted no part.

Félix picked up the negotiations, responding to Jack, "Of course, of course, you cannot be expected to pay all of the expenses. We will share the costs. But, mes amis, look at you, you are three Americans, and I am only one poor French student. Of course, I want to be most generous to my American friends. I will pay one third and you have the car for two weeks; then we trade. I get the car for one week. This is very fair, yes?" Félix smiled, his eyes sparkling with friendship and extended his hand to seal the deal.

Jack seemed happy with the arrangement. He shook Félix's hand and turned to the rest of us with a proud arrogance. The expression on his face left me with the feeling that more wheeling and dealing was on the way. I was glad not to be a part of it. Concerned that my new French friend was about to get a bad impression of my countrymen, I decided to warn Félix to be wary of Jack.

On the way back to our dorm, I cautioned Félix, "This character Jack dresses well, but he is really a shady character, *un type louche*. Don't let him trick you!'
"Not to worry for me, Richard. I know Jack. I understand him as soon as I see him. We have many Jacks in France, too, you know. This car, this car will be useful, and you, my friend, you, also, will enjoy this car." Félix assured me with his usual unbounded confidence.

A Peaceful Moment

The first time I rode in the leased car was about the same time the first snows hit the ground in early December. Jack offered to give some of us non-participants in his new leased car a ride to class one morning. The car was a Peugeot, a big car by French standards. It had a cavernous, thick metal shell lined with padded fabric. A few of us piled into the back seat enjoying the warm air that blew from the floor vents. The cushioned rear bench sat well below the small rounded windows adding to the cave like atmosphere. Narrow beams of daylight rolled across our laps, distilled into a soft white glow by the falling snow. I stretched forward leaning over the front seat as we moved along, but was only able to see a narrow slice of the road ahead. Jack navigated the barely visible streets gripping the wheel with his black leather gloves. I wished that I had gloves. As we glided along warm and comfortable, he reminded us that we could enjoy this luxurious ride frequently, for a modest sum.

The next time I rode in the car Félix was driving. I sat next to him in the front seat with a much better view of the world. He started to grumble, "This bum Jack, you know Rich, he left the gas on empty. Of course, he insisted I return the car with a full tank! *Quel idiot*! Who does he think he is, *Bon Dieu*! It's time for *Monsieur* Jack to learn how such vanity; such arrogance is rewarded in France!" Over the next six months, Félix and I took a few more trips in the Peugeot, but I never saw Jack and the car together again.

That day, we were on our way to Sue's flat. Felix had met Sue earlier while accompanying me to one of the foreign student parties. It was going to be interesting to see just how my two new friends would get along. I had a feeling that he would not be a great admirer of Colette's politics. When we arrived, the two young ladies were engaged in a heated discussion on the injustices of French society in the treatment of the poor. Félix entered with his usual panache, greeting Sue in English before I had a chance to say a word.

Sue didn't waste any time either. After a short round of hand shaking and cheek kissing, she turned her focus to Félix and spoke in French. Conveying a sense of urgency, she asked, "Have you been to the Quartier Joillet and seen the families living in those bombed out buildings across the river?" Not waiting for a reply, "Little kids playing with sticks in the piles of dirt and rocks, one toilet for an entire floor of apartments. "This is not the France that I had imagined. Don't you think something should be done to help those people?"

Félix sat down, a bit stunned. His big torso slumped back against the small chair. Then he straightened up slowly preparing to deliver his response. "It is indeed a sad affair. These poor people do need help and our government should help them. The war ended only twenty years ago. Our country is still recovering. Perhaps you have seen the tall new buildings going up across the river. Those buildings will have apartments with hot water, toilets, and even showers in each one. They will be low cost so the workers can afford to live there. It's a good first effort to address the problem." Félix leaned back again, resting on the chair.

Uncharacteristically, he did not break his attention away to scan the room and pull the rest of us into supporting his cause. He just sat there drawn in by Sue's magnetic dark brown eyes.

Colette broke in with her perspective. "It's just another bourgeois plot that will fill the pockets of wealthy land-owners. Who do you think is building those places? It is the same old aristocracy that holds all the power and wealth in this country. It's just another capitalist strategy to exploit the French worker!" She followed these comments

113

by pulling out her trusty Communist argument about the struggle between the classes, so familiar that even I understood every word she said for the next ten minutes.

 I started to imagine what the government would be like if some of my Australian mates took charge. They were all working class and fit the Communist model of the disenfranchised worker. With them in charge of the nation, it would be beer and kidney pies all around. Chaos would reign. Colette sounded like one of those Evangelical preachers who held the tent revivals back in Ohio. Her story of a struggle to free the working man didn't seem to fit anybody that I knew. It left me feeling indifferent.

My attention drifted from her words to her confident expression. Her face tightened, her cheek bones seemed to raise, a radiance lit up her eyes. She had become quite attractive. My roaming eye rolled down her body stopping to admire her firm breasts riding up against her loose sweater. I started to fantasize about spending the night in Colette's cozy bed.

When I looked over toward the kitchen, Félix and Sue were leaning across the small table almost touching. It surprised me to see Félix doing more listening than talking. He would occasionally break in with a comment like, "The state could convert the old army barracks into temporary housing," or "The students could get university credit to clean rubble from the area." His ideas made sense to me.

As the discussion continued, Félix and Sue tossed possibilities back and forth. She had not known about the low cost housing project and liked the idea. Félix came up with a few other changes like the expansion of government funded health care to include more people. While making his point sound particularly poignant, he would reach over and put his hand on Sue's shoulder, a gesture typical of the French. Unlike Jack, Sue was not bothered by this and would smile. Félix leaned forward concentrating on Sue, captivated. They continued to exchange ideas hardly aware of the presence of myself or Colette.

The German sailors I had known never talked like that with women. My Australian buddies didn't either. Even Dwayne, who really liked his girlfriend, never philosophized or mentioned helping all the bums that panhandled around King's Cross. I began to like the way Félix and Sue talked, sharing plans. The way they built on each others' ideas. It was nothing specific they were saying. Saving the world never appealed to me. It was just the connection and warmth circulating about that tiny flat as we gathered around sharing what little food and wine we had between us. They kept coming up with ways to make the world a better place. A sense of tranquility settled over me. It was that feeling of being welcome, of belonging, of being close to something of worth.

I watched my friend, Félix, rocking gently back and forth in the chair, excited by the possibilities of a better world. Sue held herself centered. Intensely focused, she sat upright as if her petit frame hardly needed the chair. They sat at the little table tossing ideas about, weaving them into a fabric of hope.

Meanwhile, I didn't say much, only the occasional "*bonne idée*", but I loved being there. It felt peaceful, vaguely familiar. I don't know why, but I began to think about those quiet moments when, as a boy back in Tennessee, I would stretch out on our living room rug to read the comic strips in the Sunday paper or play games with my brother while we listened to the radio. I felt the same sense of inner peace that I had felt back then.

Warmth

Just before Christmas break, the long awaited box of clothing arrived from California. The box contained a warm jacket, heavier pants, more socks and tee shirts. About half the clothing no longer fit as I had grown taller over the past eighteen months. Some of the pant legs didn't cover my ankles and some shirt sleeves fell short of my wrists. There were several pairs of white socks. No adult in France would be caught dead wearing white socks which belonged only as part of the elementary school girl's uniform. I felt as if I were growing out of my past.

About this time, my tooth started to ache. It hurt more and more until I could no longer ignore the pain. I went down to see the nurse in our dorm building on the first floor. She was very nice to me and wrote up a slip for me to go see a dentist. Much to my amazement, I did not have to pay for any of this treatment. Instantly, I became a big fan of the national healthcare system in France.

Mr. Arnaud, the dentist I went to see, was a friendly man with a lot of questions about *"l'Amérique"*. I had to make a few trips to see him. One day he remarked that my hands looked red from the cold. What a perceptive person, I thought to myself. Not only did I not have to pay for the dental care, he invited me to his home for dinner with his family. I was growing very fond the people in this country. Much to my surprise, Mr. Arnaud lived in a small apartment in one of the new high-rises near the university housing. It seemed a modest place for a dentist to live. That probably meant he didn't make as much money as dentists back home.

When I arrived, Mme. Arnaud was already preparing the main course of veal cutlets with a side dish of potatoes and asparagus. We settled in around the small dining table. Mr. Arnaud started off the conversation. "Tell me, Mr. Richard, what is going on with all the American soldiers headed to Vietnam? What could such a powerful nation as the United States possibly have in mind for a small country of poor people like the Vietnamese?"

It sounded like a question, but he wasn't really asking me. It was clear that Mr. Arnaud hadn't finished what he wanted to say yet. "We were there too, as colonizers. The Americans should learn from Europe's blunders. Who will your government listen to? Are they so sure of what they are doing or is it just that they are going to do whatever they feel like doing? Our opinion over here doesn't matter; is that it?"

The room fell silent and no one moved. All eyes focused on me awaiting my response. "It doesn't make any sense to me." I replied, suspecting that my hosts were expecting me to somehow be the voice of *l'Amérique.* "We have no business over there. I don't know much about politics, but it seems to me my government is acting like a big bully." The bubble burst as a quiet gush of sighs rippled through the room. Faces relaxed, smiles crossed lips. After some shuffling, Madame Arnaud returned to the kitchen and brought out the steaming plates of beef and vegetables. The rich aroma of beef juice blended into a wine and mushroom sauce drifted over the table. Everyone relaxed in anticipation. The tone shifted as a second wave of questions began.

Once again Mr. Arnaud led off the questions while the whole family zeroed in on me. "What kind of address is this that you gave me for your home in America? Such a big number! The streets must be really long there. The houses, so big too! Streets must go on for miles! And those American cars we see look gigantic with fins like rocket ships." He was smiling ear to ear.

Madame Arnaud broke in with, "American women must have an easy time with the cooking and washing. Just put

117

everything in a machine *et voila*. But those frozen meals in little metal tins, what are they doing, *mon dieux, que-est-ce qu'ils mangent ces American!*"

That comment started a barrage from all my hosts, "Les hot dogs, horrible!" the son moaned pinching his lips into a scowl. "Et le ketchup, you put the ketchup on everything *dégutant!*" I suspected none of them had ever eaten a hot dog. Yet dipping another crust of French bread in the delicious blend of beef sauce while taking a bit of asparagus from the plate in front of me, I could see their point. I wasn't about to tell them I liked ketchup.

As Mr. Arnaud continued to sketch a verbal image of a bigger-than-life vision of America, Madame Arnaud brought in a salad. She set a glass mixing bowl on the table. I watched this skilled magician whip up a salad dressing using Dijon mustard, local wine vinegar, and olive oil. Her salad dressing tasted wonderful.
By the time Madame Arnaud had cleared the plates and placed the fruit bowl before us, my hosts had developed such a joyous and fanciful image of America that I began to wonder where this place was that they described. I wanted to go there myself. Then, I realized their descriptions echoed that celluloid place created through the power of Hollywood movies and TV portrayals of the American dream.

This was my first visit to the home of a French family. I liked Mr. Arnaud, his wife, and their son. I was touched by their enthusiasm for life and the friendly reception. The food tasted delicious and the family members seemed to get along well with each other. They talked affectionately about parents and grandparents living on a nearby farm. Best of all, as I was leaving, Mr. Arnaud handed me a nice pair of winter gloves as a parting gift.

118

I walked back to the dorms that night with my hands nice and toasty in my new gloves, my coat snug around my shoulders. My belly was warm and full. The white cloud formed by my breath and the chill in my cheekbones reminded me just how cold was that night air from which I felt well shielded. I thought about how good my first few months in this land had been. I was learning more than a new language. A whole new way of seeing the world was being revealed to me. This was a safe and peaceful place. I had not seen or personally experienced any acts of violence in Dijon. Unlike Australia, rowdy public drunkenness was rare and the French behaved with compassion toward me, especially once I struggled to speak with them in their language.

My reflections on this strange new experience dulled the effects of the night wind. I thought about the way the French behaved in public. In the many small family run shops around town, owners greeted me, and each other, warmly and with respect. The ritualized politeness they used became familiar and created an oddly intimate feeling. Participating in the formalities, giving the correct responses on cue was like being in a mini play. By delivering the expected lines of *monsieur, Madame, merci, s'il vous plait, je vous en pris* and *pardon* at precisely the right moment, I could affirm my place as a well behaved participant in society.

Sitting in the cafes watching people was a way of passively connecting with the community. I had grown fond of this great sport that challenged my powers of observation. No one reacted with offense to the staring and most people actively participated. I was scrutinized as thoroughly as I scrutinized others. Each passing week, the French literature I was reading helped me discover new ways of seeing and understanding this curious land. I was even a minor celebrity of sorts being from that mythical realm of *l'Amérique.*

119

It was a very dark that night as I walked the deserted boulevard back to my dorm. The lamp posts sprayed their light in a narrow cone barely reaching the sidewalk, unable to penetrate the frozen blackness. As I scurried along, the contrast between the frosty night air and the warmth of my clothing served to heighten my awareness. I began to feel as if I were floating somewhere just above my real body, looking down on the situation. I felt deeply grateful for the experience of this evening. I found serenity in walking alone along the deserted boulevard, just happy to have discovered France. At that moment, I felt contented with just being me, the kid from *l'Amérique*. I knew that soon I would reach the harsh antiseptic lights of the dorm and this feeling would have to end.

Christmas Break in Cours
The next day, Félix made the final arrangements for me to spend Christmas with his family outside of Lyon. He would be returning home a few days early and gave me instructions to get there by train.

A French student had described to me a technique for riding the trains without paying the fare. It was a fine art requiring a solid knowledge of the layout of the train station. If one was caught in the act, the punishment was a good talking to and immediate payment of the fare. If caught a second time, the station master could make you pay a "big" fine. I never found out how much of a fine. Running low on money, I decided to give it a shot. Avoiding the controllers at the main entrance, I made my way discretely around the side of the station to an open field near the maintenance depot. I crossed a long row of tracks and walked up the far end of the platform unnoticed. From there it was just a matter of hopping on the train and dodging any conductors. This could be accomplished through judicious maneuvering between the compartments and the toilettes. It worked out pretty well from Dijon to Lyon. When I changed to one of the isolated platforms for the small local trains, there were very few passengers and a uniformed attendant standing guard. I had to pay up.

The trip was worth the fare because this was like no other train ride I had ever taken. It took longer to travel from Lyon to Félix's village of Cours than to get to Lyon from Dijon. The train stopped every five miles to pick up one or two people and their assorted bundles. On one remarkable occasion, we arrived at an intersection where a country road crossed the tracks between two steep hills. The train actually stopped and the conductor got out. Walking in front of the train, he looked both ways before starting the engine rolling again.

It was a beautiful region, more mountainous than the area outside of Dijon. As the train traveled further away from the larger town of Roanne, we passed more open woodlands and groups of farm houses clustered amid the rolling countryside. A number of long narrow brick buildings built right on the river's edge looked like textile mills. We headed northwest where the hills grew steeper. Snow lay in scattered patches across the landscape. Tall fir trees and thick grass covered the slopes. There weren't any castles along the tracks like those found in Burgundy, although many of the farms had clearly been there for centuries.

Félix met me at the train station in Cours around mid-afternoon the day before Christmas. He was the same jubilant fellow that I had seen just a few days earlier. But here, in his village, he glowed with confidence like the master of ceremonies at a three ring circus. Vigorously shaking my hand he declared, *"Mon cher ami Richard!* Welcome to my marvelous little village of Cours." Pride radiated from his eyes.

As we walked from the train station towards Félix's parents' home, everyone we met stopped to greet us. Félix introduced me to the villagers as *"Je vous presente, mon ami, le grand American, Richard."* For a brief moment, I would feel important as villagers smiled warmly shaking my hand. But in short order they turned to Félix, directing the conversation to local matters. I could only understand bits and pieces of the exchanges. Someone's apple trees had not done well. The stone walls were settling in another's wine cellar. At times, I understood nothing of what was said. The language they spoke shifted to a jumble of noise. . It didn't even sound like French, becoming incomprehensible.

Whether or not I understood did not matter, for once a conversation got underway, these folks became very serious and completely ignored me. I could have been a tree or a goat. This was fine with me, as I became a fly on Félix's shoulder. Free to watch through this invisible veil of my insignificance, I got to glimpse what it might be like to live here, to have been raised here.

Félix's family home was near the center of town. It was one of those houses with high stone walls and a front window located well above the street. Inside, the floors were made of a heavy oak, almost black. Tall dark mahogany sideboards and display cabinets lined the dining room. The kitchen was not large, yet uncluttered. It contained some cast iron pots and pans, a few utensils, the essentials. A narrow wooden staircase that looked centuries old led up to the bedrooms on the second floor. The dining room, directly across from the kitchen, was spacious; a large table filled the room. It was a comfortable home and prominently located only a few blocks from the town's center.

Félix's family welcomed me enthusiastically and I immediately felt at ease. Félix's father had the same charming manner as his son. A successful man, he was running the family owned textile mill, carrying on a business started by Félix's grandfather. Félix's mother came from the kitchen to greet me even though she was busy. She showed me to my room and returned to preparing the evening meal.

His parents left the job of playing host to Félix. Since he loved to talk and always had a lot to say, I did not have to entertain as the American guest. It was a relief to know that I was not going to be the focus of a lot of questions. Not having to constantly struggle with the language, I could relax.

We gathered that evening around the big dining room table for the aperitif. I had my choice of liqueurs, various Sherries, whiskeys, or cognacs. Wonderful odors drifted out of the kitchen. I began to look forward to another terrific meal.

After a few drinks, we sat down to dinner and I tasted live oysters for the first time. Prepared still attached to their shells, they were served cold in light lemony salt water. It took a little getting used to as they still wiggled a bit, or so I imagined. The sauce reminded me of ocean water. When washed down with a chilled Chenin Blanc, they weren't half bad.

Next we were served *paillasson,* a potato dish that looked like a pie with a golden top layer. This was followed by a salad made of garden greens and mushrooms. A mellow Beaujolais accompanied the tray of local cheeses that arrived. We finished with a fresh fruit platter and were ready to wash down the meal with the *digestif.*

Félix's father proposed a special drink, described as an *eau de ville.* This brew was made from a local farmer's pear harvest. This stuff was eighty-proof fire water. The special flavor lovingly described in all its uniqueness was lost on my pallet as it burned its way down my throat like a flow of molten lava. I stopped trying to speak, my head began to float. I leaned back in the chair. My warm belly pressed

123

comfortably against the lower edge of the table. After the
initial shock passed, I began to think it was going to be a
most enjoyable evening.

The family talked about Félix's plans for the future. He
was about to graduate and move forward with a career in
business. His older brother was already running a textile
business in the south of France. He was so busy managing
the place that he had no chance to come home for Christmas. There was vague talk of Félix considering marriage
plans. I got the impression that Félix was not quite ready to
commit to anything just yet and preferred to enjoy his
freedom a while longer.

Again, all the attention was directed to Félix and local is-
sues while generally ignoring my presence. This pattern
persisted throughout my visit. Cours occupied the center of
the universe for its inhabitants. Their world was less than
flat; it covered an area no greater than twenty square miles.
Yet, they acted out their emotions with the passion of
kings ruling vast territories. Everything they had to say
took on a quality of being extremely important, each decision deadly serious.

For them, I vanished, a vague non-threatening presence.
For me, it was thrilling to be able to vicariously participate
in life here. The Catholic school was planning a Nativity
play. Someone's honey had turned out more sweetly perfumed and particularly tasty that year. I strained to understand, uncertain of what was being said.

Midnight Mass
On Christmas Eve, the family invited me to go with them
to midnight mass. We walked a short distance through cold
snow flurries to the town center where the village church
stood. Once inside, the soft lighting reflected off the red
and yellow panes of the imposing stained glass windows

that adorned the thick walls. As people entered, the sound of their shoes clicking against the floor echoed overhead, amplified by the vaulted ceiling. Every tapping of heels against the stone, every jingle of keys, the rumbling of voices, all rose up and echoed above in a thunderous roar. Gradually, silence settled over the congregation, an intimidating silence enlarged and deepened by the expansive nave.

I stood next to Félix bending a bit at the knees, trying not to be too conspicuous. The priest came out from a side door then climbed up on a platform. He gestured with his arms and everyone sat down. Good, I thought. Now, I can settle down and listen. It made me a little nervous when the priest started to speak in Latin. I wasn't going to know what was going on.

Then, much to my surprise, everybody stood up. I almost remained seated and had to hurry. Just as I found a comfortable stance, everyone sat down again. Every couple of minutes the assembly would get up and sit down leaving me a half step behind. At one point, I had noticed people starting to move and stood up quickly trying to get in sync. Suddenly, I found myself standing all alone facing the priest. Everyone else had risen just slightly in order to kneel on the wooden platforms attached to the pews in front of them. I wasn't feeling invisible anymore.
After twenty minutes of constant movement, I started to get the hang of it and was cutting down my lag time. Then, an extraordinary event began. A group of three religious men appeared in the back of the church. They were dressed in thick white robes with big red crosses on the front panel. The robes were embellished with lots of silver needlework. They wore tall white pointed caps covered with thick silver threaded crosses and silver braiding around the edges. They carried two dome shaped gold vessels suspended on long chains, one in each hand. Smoke rose from s-shaped slots in the vessels. Like three ivory chess pieces, they

sauntered slowly toward the alter swinging the vessels back and forth spreading smoke across the nave. As they moved forward, they chanted in voodoo-like voices.

They floated slowly down the isle, their monotone Latin incantations mingled with the perfumed musky odor of incense, casting a mesmerizing spell. Just as these ghostly clerics reached, our pew, time was momentarily suspended. The past and present seemed to converge for me. I felt transported to a timeless realm.

Surely, similarly dressed priests had enacted this ritual for centuries in village churches all over France. Like the many others who had experienced it, this magic ritual overwhelmed me. It was just for a brief instant in time, but I would always remember being caught in that moment. Mass eventually came to an end and everyone began leaving the church. Outside, Félix was quickly surrounded by people kissing him or shaking his hand. He seemed to know everyone and they were all inviting us to stop by their homes that evening. Félix kept nodding his head promising to visit. It was one o'clock in the morning

We hiked across the cold pavement to the first of several homes. Inside, the dining room beckoned, warm and well lighted. The table was neatly arranged with various dishes. Platters of *pâté de foie gras*, Brie, and goat cheeses had been placed on the table next to bowls containing nuts and candies. Thin baguettes cut in half were distributed over the white tablecloth. An enticing large chocolate cake had been placed in prominence in the center of the table. It was shaped like a log, its rings interwoven with light brown layers of cream. All sorts of liqueurs, cognacs, wines and other bottles of unknown beverages were bunched together on a side cart.

We sat at the table as I listened to Félix speaking, sometimes in serious tones, at others jubilant while outlining stories with his hands floating through the air. Our hosts joined in commenting and gesturing with equal enthusiasm. It was difficult for me to understand the discussions since several people would be talking at the same time. However, it was easy to feel the fellowship binding all present together. This sense of community, of belonging, was comforting even though I did not really belong. I was surprised to experience a sense of kinship in the presence of this many people, considering that I had rebelled against participation in any kind of group during my high school days back in California.

The drinks flowed generously. So many tasty snacks washed down with wines that only got better from glass to glass. I was getting pretty tipsy, but the continual intake of food kept me steady. Félix and I moseyed from house to house. Families greeted us with an abundance of food and drink. Lots of animated conversation invigorated the brightly lighted homes and bountiful tables of our hosts. Then back we went into the cold night. Each trip into the crisp air became a little less bothersome as our stomachs filled to the brim. At last, around four in the morning, we returned home to soft beds and sleep.

Christmas morning, I learned, much to my delight, that the French do not exchange gifts on that day. My resources were almost depleted making the purchase of gifts impossible. Fortunately for me, Félix knew of my financial situation. We spent a quiet day, in part recovering from the night before. After a few late day visits and a restful evening, darkness settled over the holiday.

The next morning, Félix's father gave me a big wireless radio as a parting gift. Perhaps he thought I would like to listen to events in my homeland, or maybe it was a symbolic token of his own spirit of adventure. I tucked it under my arm and headed off toward the train station. I must have looked a bit like a parting Charlie Chaplin. I felt like jumping and clicking my heels together to pantomime my high spirits.

A Winter of Work

Upon my return, I headed straight for the student employment office to look for work. The first job available was at *Lamartine*, a small hotel tucked away at the end of a short alley in the old part of town. It was a job working the night desk. There were not a lot of visitors to the place during the week and almost no one arrived after ten in the evening. The reception desk faced a double front door. The lower half of the door was made of paneled wood and the upper an array of ten-inch square glass panes with a view onto the stone courtyard. Opening the door by its long brass handle felt like entering a castle. I loved the hotel.

On the right side of the desk two tall doors led to a small office with a couch. I could use the couch to read and sleep while getting paid. It was a good job. Unfortunately, it did not pay enough to allow for any savings. So I looked for a second job.

The student employment office found me a temporary job working for a local movie theater. That is how I met Mohammed, a young man from Algeria. He had dark skin and eyes that were almost black. Compared to my blue eyes and light brown hair, we made an unlikely pair of Roman soldiers.

The Olympia Theater was holding a grand opening of the film "The Fall of the Roman Empire" that week. They decided to hire some students to promote the movie. Our job was to dress up like Roman Soldiers and walk up and down the main streets shouting "Come one and all to see The Fall of the Roman Empire."

The theater gave us authentic looking outfits. We wore tights, pleated skirts with alternating cloth and metal slats, a breast plate that looked like steel. We placed Centurion tin helmets on our heads with red plumes arched above. The helmet's padded metal plates flapped against our cheeks. We carried wooden poles painted to look like spears.

Mohammed and I stomped around town shouting, waiving our spears, and generally entertaining passers-by. The more we got into the spirit, the bolder we became, marching into stores and improvising for the customers. Mohammed turned out to be quite a prankster as we faked fights and asked people for their Roman Citizen cards. We even got our picture in the paper. We looked more like an international brigade, a Nordic invader accompanying a Moorish tribesman.

A few weeks after this acting job ended, I landed a new second job as a waiter/busboy in a small family run restaurant, *Le Petit Chatelet,* a *pension famille.* It finally became possible to save a few francs.

The concept of *pension famille* was unknown to me before this job. The same people came to eat there every day. They paid by the week. The menu was set each mid-day, the same for everyone. I worked the lunch meal, allowing me to continue my night job at the hotel.

The restaurant's clientele consisted largely of single people and a few elderly couples with one or two tables set aside for the occasional walk-in. Situated on a modest square in a neighborhood away from the center, there were few new faces appearing in the restaurant.

Madame Latousse, the wife of the owner, orchestrated the lunchtime event while Monsieur Latousse cooked and managed the kitchen. They had a young daughter, about five years old, who wandered between the tables and the kitchen. A nice fringe benefit of the job was the free lunch every day. The meals generally consisted of four courses and were always first rate as far as I was concerned.

Madame Latousse, a big-boned woman, spoke in a loud voice letting all present know who was in charge. Once the guests had meandered in and filled the half dozen tables, she would pass the plates across the kitchen counter with a big smile on her face and swing into action.
Ostensibly talking to me, in a booming voice that filled the cramped salon, she would call out,
"Take this plate to that fat lady in the purple dress at the small table in the corner"
"This plate goes to the bald-headed man in the checkered suit at that middle table."
"Take this plate to the widow Arlene over there in the brown dress."
"Here is a plate for the man with the cane; remind him to use his napkin."
"Bring this dish to the skinny professor with the glasses."
"Tell Monsieur Rouault to please remove his hat!"

Much to my surprise, customers reacted very little to the comments of Madame Latousse. Surely, they had heard it all and long ago accepted the characterizations. Some even appeared to chuckle to themselves, passive participants in this odd game.

Her abrasive and uninhibited way of pointing out the ec-centricities of her customers surprised me in its frankness. Yet such bold outspokenness and the acquiescing to it in-duced a curious sense of community. Everyone tolerated their treatment with a good degree of stoicism.

I thought of people stereotyping me as the tall American. This behavior resonated nebulously with experiences in my childhood. It reminded me a little of our Italian neighborhood of East Grease back in Rochester where you had to be careful as a kid. If you acted badly, one of the other parents on the block was just as likely to scold you as your own mother. A kid could get a reputation that could become hard to escape.

The desire to earn more money slowly crept to the top of my priority list. My French was improving more from speaking on the job every day than from attending classes. No one kept track of my attendance at the university. I would not get kicked out of school for absenteeism. The only tests in the program took place at the end of the school year. My student card would continue to be valid for the cheap meals and I could continue to live in the dorms. Why not take another job to build up some serious savings?

Once again, the student employment office came through for me. A night shift job opened up at a warehouse of *Prisunique,* a large grocery store chain. The hours were from eleven p.m. to seven a.m. The night shift supervisor hired me the very same day. That night I became a man on the run from one job to the next.

It took some fast talking to try to convince the owner of Lamartine to let me take the afternoon shift ending at ten p.m. He agreed. The only part of that job I was going to miss was the Friday night shift which was a mixed blessing at best.

That was the night the farm boys came to town to party with their girlfriends. Those country boys didn't see much cash cross over their hands, swollen red from labor. They would seek out budget hotels like *Lamartine*. The couples stumbled through the door wrapped in each others arms, hips pressed together. Smelling of wine, clothes hanging loose, buttons undone, their eyes sparkled with anticipation. Long days toiling in the fields gave those boys lots of stamina. The hotel came alive with moaning and groaning.

The thin walls between the office and adjacent rooms rattled in sync with the ruckus. It was fun to listen to all that pleasure, but a little unnerving and hard to sleep. I could forget about studying.

When the afternoon shift ended, it took about thirty minutes to rush across town to the warehouse. I whipped through the snowy streets which were abandoned at that hour, arriving in time to eat a bite, punch in, and stack boxes. At seven the next morning, I made the long journey up hill to my dorm room.

After a few hours sleep, off I went again to wait tables at *Le Petit Chatelet*. From the restaurant, I occasionally attended one of the afternoon classes. Mostly, I headed off for the cafés on the Place Darcy to relax and visit with friends before my shift at *Lamartine*.

This frantic pace gradually exhausted me. After a few weeks of biking back to the dorms in the morning, the long uphill ride grew so difficult that I found myself pushing my rickety old bike half way home. I grew tired of the dorms and wanted to be closer to town. Besides, most of the Americans lived in the dorms. They always wanted me to join them, to speak English, and pretend we were in the States. I decided to move out of the university housing.

Eleanor and the Devants
Apart from Sue, the only other American I met who did not live in the dorms was Eleanor. She possessed a wholesome all-American kind of charm. I could see a Fourth of July parade float gliding by with her in the center wearing a ribbon over her shoulder that read "Miss Apple Queen". The loose cut and primary colors of her conservative cloth-

132

ing clashed with the tapered tailoring and nuanced shades of the French outfits. The frocks hung from her shoulders like a sandwich board that read, "American girl". Whether Eleanor felt indifferent or was simply unaware of her appearance, I never knew. Yet, Eleanor held a strong confident presence among the foreign students, always friendly and open. There was an uninhibited integrity in her American manner. I liked her from our first meeting.

Eleanor rarely stayed after classes to gossip in the cafés with the other Americans. She lived in a village on a hill at the edge of town called Talant. Like Sue and me, she was financing her stay in France without help from her parents. Eleanor worked as an *au pair* for a French family. The job was that of a live-in babysitter of sorts who helped out with other family chores. *Au pairs* were treated as part of the family. She lived with Dr. Devant, head of surgery in the local hospital, his wife, and their three children.

I met her in one of the linguistics classes and was impressed by her willingness to speak French. On a few occasions, I had complained to her about the other Americans distain for the French and their refusal to use the language. She knew I was becoming disillusioned with dorm life. When Eleanor told me that Dr. Devant had offered to rent me a room, I jumped at the chance.

The monthly cost was about the same as the dorms. At first, I figured Dr. Devant must like having Americans around. Turned out, he also could use some help and threw in a few chores for me. I had to refill the oil heater regularly. It was on the second story in the children's nursery next to my room. I also took out the trash. These were small requests and the family was very kind in welcoming me in to share their home.

Talant perched precariously on a hill overlooking the town of Dijon. It was a little more than half as far from the town

133

center as the route I biked each day from the dorms. The street leading to Talant was not as steep either. A narrow two lane road wound up through the countryside to Talant between a patchwork of small family farms.

The Devant's home was nestled in the center of a side street on the outermost edge of the village facing the city. It was an ancient country manor. An old stone structure on the outside, it had been completely remodeled inside. Reaching the front door through the narrow streets, any view of the surrounding farmland was obscured. Once through the home's courtyard and inside the house, a stunning panorama opened up. A long row of French doors lined the far side of the living room, revealing a magnificent vista of green slopes and the city's skyline. One could see cathedral towers springing up here and there among the rows of black slate and red tiled rooftops that lined Dijon's boulevards.

My lodging was on the second floor with the same wonderful view. It had one twin bed and an armoire for my clothes. Not much bigger than the cabins on the German freighters, it must have served as a maid's quarters at one time. To reach the bedroom, I had to pass through part of the children's nursery where light floated in through large windows that opened onto a narrow balcony that overlooked the enclosed courtyard.

Dr. Devant and his wife took me in without the usual fanfare about l'Amérique. Eleanor lived in one of the rooms downstairs and kept busy helping Madame Devant in the kitchen. Eleanor spent a lot of time with the children, twin girls and an older boy. The three children filled their days attending school during the day and doing homework most of the afternoon. They had little time to play.

The twins were about ten years old and fought constantly. They took opposing sides on every possible subject. One liked horses, the other hated horses. One liked reading romance novels while the other only liked science. The boy, who was about twelve, avoided them altogether pursuing his passion for building model ships in his few free moments.

Meanwhile, I raced from job to job only coming back to Talant to sleep in the mornings before heading to the restaurant. The one break came on Sundays. All businesses closed Sundays. The sound of church bells rose from every corner of the city parceling out the Sabbath. Dr. Devant gathered his extended household together on this day for a ritualistic afternoon walk in one of the many surrounding woodlands.

Both he and his wife possessed a keen knowledge of the region. They could identify any flower or plant we came across on our walks. These were long walks, typically lasting a few hours and covering several miles. Often, we would stop to study some vista. Dr Devant instructed us in the region's history. He would point out ancient ruins in the area, talk about the battles fought in a valley or identify a Roman aqueduct that joined two hills.

Frequently, I was invited to Sunday dinners with the family. These meals were not the typical four course sit-downs to with I had become familiar. Monique, his wife, would serve small quantities of a lean meat dish with a few boiled vegetables. Most surprising to me, no wine was provided with the meal. We drank mineral water instead. Healthy as it was, I almost always felt hungry afterwards.
As time went on, I realized the degree to which Dr. Devant was a frugal man. After my first shower, he instructed me in the art of washing efficiently. To properly clean oneself while conserving water, I was to run the water briefly, just long enough to get wet. Shut the water off and scrub my body well with soap. Then turn the water back on just long enough to rinse. All done.

135

Refilling the heating oil got to me as well. He always bought just enough and we would run low as the end of the month approached. I eventually learned to use it sparingly, waiting until the stove had completely cooled down before refueling. I became skilled at stretching the oil supply over a few extra days before a new reserve arrived.

Vidal

Life perked up for all the English speaking foreign students when Vidal and his girlfriend Hana rolled into Dijon early that spring. He was over six feet tall, like me, and even thinner. I had never before seen a young black man like Vidal. The complexion of the African Americans I had known back in California resembled milk chocolate while Vidal was as dark as a moonless night. He spoke with a smooth English accent while words floated out of his mouth in soothing tones. He walked using long strides, his back straight as an arrow.

I struck up a casual friendship with him shortly after our first meeting at the student restaurant. I loved watching him glide gracefully around the cafés, his head floating through the crowd like a giraffe above the tree tops. Hana was his opposite with a voluptuous body, pale white skin, bleach blonde hair and a German accent when she spoke English. Neither could speak French very well. They never seemed to attend our University classes, but Hana somehow arranged to take a room in the girl's dormitory and Vidal stayed there every night, against school rules.
I tried to copy his walk, but could only admire his speech.

When Vidal spoke, his gestures were slow and elegant. Speaking with the confidence of a diplomat, he manipulated conversations to follow his measured pace. Most extraordinary of all, he had a gift for inspiring people to give him money. For me, Vidal was living art in motion.

136

One afternoon while walking to the center of town from my job as a waiter at *Le Petit Chatelet*, I ran into Vidal heading toward the *Place Darcy*. "Hi, Richard, been looking for you, mate. I'm off to the *Café du Nord,* come on; I'll buy you a drink."

We paused after entering the café as Vidal's eyes scanned across the noisy crowd and raising splinters of smoke. His attention zeroed in on Roger, a well-dressed young man from Chicago, who kept company exclusively with the other American students. In this rare instance, Roger was in the café without his mentor Jack at his side. He sat alone in the far back corner of the café looking a little forlorn. We worked our way over to his table, Vidal leading, me following, concentrating on holding my back upright as we approached.

"Hey, Roger. Here by yourself, mate? We been lookin for you. Be a good bloke and buy me a glass of wine. You'll be glad of it. I'm going to offer you a rare opportunity from my Africa." Vidal pulled back a chair without waiting for a reply. I sat down even though they both ignored me. Sure enough, Roger bought Vidal a glass of wine. I had to pay for my own coffee.

"That's a fine suit your sportin' mate? Must be more o'those quality threads you blokes from Chicago tapped into." A smug confidence came over Roger's face as he straightened up in the chair.

"Hey mate, remember my family business in Africa. I told you all o 'bout it, right? Well, I wanta cut you in on a great deal. I'm waiting on a big check from Lagos. You know how it is. There's official reviews, delays in Lagos to assess the financials of a major family like mine. You see, mate, the colonials passed on a lotta regulations for my people. Guess what, though, I just got word. All that cash'll be freed up soon, very soon, mate, …very soon."

Vidal paused, leaning slightly closer to Roger. "I'll tell you what, Roger. I know you're not a racist like those other guys in America. So I'm gunna pay you some major interest if you loan me two hundred franks 'til a week or so. You take care of your African friend Vidal and he'll put some profit in your hand soon, some real money, mate!" Vidal leaned back in his chair casually, looked around the café ignoring Roger and waited.

After a few drawn-out minutes of awkward silence, Roger squirmed and tapped a finger against his glass of beer. He looked up at Vidal and began to speak, a strained air of shrewdness resonated in his voice. "If I do give you two hundred francs, when do you expect to be able to pay me back? How much interest will you pay…. double my money?" He took a swig of his beer and returned the glass to the table with an unsettled hand.

"Come on Roger, I just said I know you're not out to take advantage of your black brother, now don't prove me wrong here, mate. Don't confound the meaning of my generosity; I know you're a smart businessman. So I'll give you two hundred and fifty francs. Now that's a bloody good return on a loan of only a week or so. You guna be feelin' smart, mate… American business man of international stature like yourself. It's a deal you'll be braggin' 'bout to your friends."

It was almost three in the afternoon and I was going to be late for work at *L'Hotel Lamartine's* as the desk clerk. I got up and nodded goodbye to them, but neither noticed. Just as I moved for the door, I caught sight of Roger reaching in his vest pocket. He pulled out his wallet and handed Vidal a wad of money while glancing my way, his mouth drawn tight in an unconvincing smile.

Vidal seemed the conquering hero to me. Over the next few weeks, I spent the occasional afternoon with him and Hana in their dorm room. However, I took care never to carry money when I dropped in to see them.

"Hi rich, want some coffee?" Hana asked when I stopped by one afternoon. She took a thin line of instant coffee from a folded piece of white paper. Using the crease in the paper as a funnel, she carefully tipped the line of instant coffee into a cup filled with hot tap water. My eyes moved from her steady hands to her pale breasts bulging out of a strained black blouse, then down the curve of her skin tight red slacks. Hana looked pretty inviting. I imagined myself strolling along the dock, Hana on my arm, as my former shipmates looked on with envy.

My eyes quickly turned away as Vidal entered the room. Hana directed her attention to him. "Look, here, Vidal …that's all the coffee. Did you get tickets to the student restaurant for tonight with the money I gave you? What you been doin' all day?" She sat in the small metal chair, her eyes fixed on Vidal. He moved slowly to the desk stretching out a hand. "Here's for you woman." Vidal handed her two crumpled tickets and turned to me. "Hey, mate, got any meal tickets for me tomorrow? We could use a few."

Before I could respond, Hana cut in, staring at Vidal "Leave him be, I went to see the lady today. It's all set for next week if you got the money. I did my part, …went there by myself. You set up the train to London yet? Got the money?"

"Where did you go, ….what lady?" I asked.

Hana didn't answer, her eyes stayed on Vidal who ignored her gaze. "It's in the works woman, I'm consolidating business. Now, give us a few francs for my affairs" Vidal smiled. Hanna's glare turned cold as she pulled a ten frank note from her purse and tossed it across the table without saying a word.

A few days later, the inevitable finally happened, Vidal caught up with me as I headed down a side street to work at *L'Hotel Lamartine*. He put his hand on my shoulder and smiled. "You've got to come see me and Hana in London, mate. A world traveler like yourself can't afford to miss out on it" His hand on my shoulder felt heavy. "I know you'll love it there, mate. Hana, she has some sweet German girlfriends in London who would be aching to meet a fine young American bloke like yourself."

I began to feel nervous, unsure. "I don't know Vidal, the only Germans I ever knew were sailors and the only German women they ever talked about wanted cash in advance... A visit to London does sound great, though."
"Yah, you'll love it, mate. We got a little place in Soho, in the middle of a lot o' hot London night life. You can stay with us, all cozy, all expenses covered mate."

Pushing both hands deep into my pockets, I felt the ten franc note I was saving and clutched it in my right hand. "Sure Vidal, it all sounds good." I tried to smile, feeling a little dizzy.
His expression changed, more serious now, he looked troubled. "Listen Richard, it's tough being away from London. You got to struggle just to get some food here in France. When I get back to London with Hana, we'll have a good life. We'll be living in comfort, you'll see. You know what I mean, mate. Right now, we need some money to pay for that dorm room." He stepped a bit closer and laid his hand on my shoulder.

"Hana, she likes you, mate. Always saying what a nice bloke you are. She's right. You're a good bloke, come on now; loan me fifty franks to help us cover expenses. I'll make it right when you're in London. I know you got the money. I know you can do it. You'll be proud to say you helped out your African brother, Vidal. You know you will mate."

Tightening my grip on that ten franc note, I could feel myself losing ground and decided to try my own hard luck story. "Hey Vidal, you see me workin' three jobs. I'm strugglin' myself to pay the bills. You really think I can lend you money?" My squeaky voice sounded pitiful. My mind was drifting out of focus. The faint rumble of a distant past was pulling me back.

My father's voice echoed up from the recesses of my mind "I am going to teach you boys a lesson," he had said as he reached down and took our toy cars from our little hands. My brother and I looked at each other, shocked and dismayed. What kind of lesson could God, our father, want us to learn? Why did we have to give him our sleek metal cars? He turned, walked across the lawn, and handed our cars to two grungy looking boys on the sidewalk. We knew those boys. They lived in that crumbly little house at the end of our street, the one with all the junk on the lawn and no curtains, the one by the railroad tracks.

My brother and I looked at each other, still stunned. We liked our toy cars. We watched those kids walking down the street carrying our cars. Those were mean kids. They had once threatened to beat me up. My brother and I did not like them.

"Listen closely, boys. It's your responsibility to be generous in life and help those more needy than yourselves. Sometimes it hurts to give up your things. Now, remember this lesson boys; it's important to understand. People are basically good and deserve our help." Dad's autocratic voice echoed through time and space.
"That's the point mate," Vidal continued. "You got three jobs to keep you in the cash. I got Hana to look after and I

know you wanta be good to her. You know how the girls need us blokes to take care o 'em. She's so fond a you, mate."

"All I got is ten francs and that's my food and café money." I mumbled as my hand involuntarily came out of my pocket, opening to expose the crumpled bill. Vidal plucked it from my palm. He held it out with his right hand as he smoothed out the wrinkles between the long thin fingers of his left hand. "Mate, is that all you got for me? Hana's gonna feel sad. But, hey, thanks mate, you're a good bloke, for sure." His parting words provided no comfort.

"Sorry mate," I whimpered, feeling stunned and angry with myself as I watched Vidal disappear down the street. Near the end of that week, Hana showed up in the *Café du Nord*, early afternoon. She was all smiles. I was sitting by myself that day in a half empty café. Hana joined me and put her hand on my arm, "I'd like you to know, Rich, that today we can celebrate, buy me a white wine. It's done, I'm liberated, … on to better things."

Hana smelled good and looked even better, glowing with an air of satisfaction. I bought her the wine, curious to hear why she was so happy. "Where did all that joy come from?" I asked.

Hana sipped the glass of wine slowly, "I saw the lady yesterday. Her mood turned briefly dark, "Let's say, …from nothing comes nothing…." her expression tightened; her eyes revealed a flash of sadness. But, the joy quickly resurfaced, "and she gave me new life." Hana looked pleased with herself again, but, I could tell Hana was not about to fill me in on the details.

The following week, Vidal and Hana vanished. They had passed through Dijon shaking up our little group of foreign students. The two of them blew out of town as suddenly as

142

they had arrived, leaving a swirl of angry Americans holding a stack of bad debt. I counted among those who had to face the fact; we would never be repaid. However, unlike my fellow Americans, I felt that I had paid a fair price for my education. I had mastered a new way of strutting into a café that made me feel sophisticated. From then on, I walked tall and was proud of a new found stride.

Turmoil and Change

Working alone a lot of the time in a warehouse full of food, was just too great a temptation for me. I began to eat some of the food I was supposed to be stacking. By combining these snacks with my daily lunch Le Petit Chatelet, I did not need to spend any money or time at the student restaurant.

The months of racing around got to me. One night, I slipped into the basement of one of the dorms and "borrowed" some poor unknowing student's Moped, a motorized bicycle, leaving my dilapidated old bike in its place. Driving this motorized bicycle between jobs saved time and effort. I would then stash it in a park near Talant in the early morning hours. This took some the pressure off and bought me a little extra time.

I had backpedaled, turning my life into a deal with the devil. There was no easy escape from all the stress. Swapping poverty for this new set of problems didn't help much. I felt very guilty for having taken the Moped. Worrying about being caught and thrown out of France or worse weighed on me. I grew paranoid and was sure people knew I was eating up the company profits on the job. Every time I faced the night manager, it was impossible to look him in the eye. He must know. All my co-workers' eyes were surely focused on my pockets full of food wrappers.

In short order, leading this life of crime while dashing from job to job became too much: one morning my nerves cracked. Attempting to clear my conscience, I returned the Moped. I resolved to quit taking food from the warehouse as I pushed my old bike back up the hill to Talant.
Once back in Talant, I collapsed onto my bed, exhausted.

A few hours later, I was unable to get out of bed and go to work. It had all been just too much. After coming in to examine me, Dr. Devant concluded that I was suffering from mononucleosis. A big name like that had to be a terrible disease. He called all my employers to inform them that I would not be coming to work for a while.

The next two weeks were spent resting, eating soup and struggling to walk around the nursery. When I finally did get back on my feet, there was no way I was going return to racing between all those jobs.

I quit working at the warehouse and the hotel. I took a part-time job in a lumber yard moving boards around during the morning hours. The lumber yard was just at the bottom of the hill from Talant. The one job I kept was at Le Petit Chatelet. I loved working for Madame Latousse and enjoyed Mr. Latousse's cooking. My afternoons remained free, permitting me to attend classes and hang out in the cafes. My conscience no longer troubled me.

Talant was located on the same side of town as Sue's apartment. I used to pass right by her place every day on my way to the restaurant. Occasionally, I would stop to talk and visit. Some nights, I stayed in the flat with Colette.

During my visits, Sue often reminisced about Israel. She kept talking about how beautiful it was and how much she loved her summer there. She described life in the kibbutz with great affection. Every once in a while Sue would speak Hebrew to me, teaching me a few of the words she had learned while attending language classes in the Ulpan program. She even gave me information from an Israeli international student organization on how to attend an Ulpan.

I was hooked. By the end of winter, I had saved up enough money to travel to Israel the coming summer. I began to look into ships that went there in early June.

Around the time that the snow began to melt revealing dead grass, yellow and crushed from a long winter, Colette broke the news to me. She felt she could no longer sleep with me. She had decided to dedicate herself more completely to the Trotsky cause. She hinted that this was now going to include the application of her sexual favors to the advancement of the movement. I took the news calmly and bravely. Unsavory visions of her hugging factory workers with dirty hands wearing drab blue denim jackets flashed across my mind. I couldn't shake my twisted image of her pressed naked against a fat, cigar smoking, union boss she had invited into her bed just to convert him to the cause.

If she was really willing to make such an extraordinary sacrifice, then I was more than ready to bow out of our sexual relationship. I still liked her. Besides, I felt that she had been very generous towards me up to that point. She never promised me anything, never expressed much emotion.

Afternoons at the cafes provided cheap entertainment especially as the winter dissolved and patches of flowers sprang up in the fields. The parks began to turn green again.

In the cafés, there was that occasional irritation of running into Jack. He always asked where he could find Félix and "his car". I knew that I could probably find Félix, but the car was a different matter. Félix was moving it around, loaning it out to his buddies and parking it in a different location almost every night.

Jack was no angel and I was not about to help him. If he could only master a few words of French after almost nine months in the country, he did not deserve my respect. Maybe Félix should not have weaseled him out of the car completely. Still, Felix had little choice, I felt sure that if Jack ever got the car back, he would have done the same, or worse, to Félix. I wanted nothing to do with Jack. His karmic boomerang had swung full circle smacking him square in the wallet.

The Summer Ahead

Gradually, barren tree branches sprouted new limbs covered in small green leaves; grass broke through the hard ground everywhere. The tables of cafés mushroomed onto sidewalks as days grew longer and evenings warmer. The University scheduled final exams for mid-May.

Although, I had learned enough French to carry on a conversation and understand much of what I heard, my knowledge of grammar was weak. There were too many messy verb conjugations. Trying to remember what tenses to use in which kinds of sentences got muddled in my mind. After all, I never thought about grammar in my every day conversations.

What about the many French novels still to be read? I had stopped reading when I began to work full time. There was little likelihood that I would pass the exams. I decided not to take them. Still, I had not given up.
After a year in Dijon, I felt that I had found a new home. This country, this town in particular, held me in its spell. I wanted more time here. All the other Americans had made plans for their journey home, including Sue.

Even though Félix was moving on to begin his career in the textile industry and no one I knew was coming back, I thought the right thing for me would be to return the next year. For the first time, I felt a sense of personal worth. I was someone who had aroused curiosity, even affection, in the French people. Dijon welcomed me assigning me this special identity, an authority, a spokesperson for *l'Amérique.*

In spite of my love of Dijon, spring was in the air. The temptation to strike out on a new adventure pulled at my coat sleeve. The hunger to explore and curiosity also were still strong forces driving me. I needed to test my limits. I wrote to the Israeli youth cultural organization and was accepted for their summer program. I settled on spending three months of the summer in Israel.

By spring, Eleanor and I had become pretty good friends. She often talked to me about life with her family in Spain. Her father, although civilian, ran the commissary on a US Air Force base in the suburbs of Madrid. She was heading back there at the end of May and invited me to spend some time with her family on the base.

I also considered some of good old Arnfin's projects. He was one of my Norwegian buddies, a long boney fellow with one of my old problems; his clothes didn't quite fit. He didn't quite fit. Arnfin raced around Dijon on his bicycle looking like Ichabod chased by the Headless Horseman. He cooked up unusual trips such as the one to Salzburg during Easter holiday to watch the monks celebrate.

That Sunday afternoon, they climbed to the top of the bell tower in Salzburg's main cathedral carrying bags of rose petals. Some carried red rose petals, others white rose petals. They proceeded to empty the sacks in tandem onto the town square below. As the church bells rang, a great red and white cloud floated down from the heavens. That's

147

how Arnfin described it, anyway. Regrettably, I had passed on that trip,

However, he did convince me to join him at La Camargue in late June. According to Arnfin, it had remained a most sacred place for the gypsies of Europe since the fourth century. Every June, thousands of gypsies from France, Spain, Italy and even Romania would gather there to celebrate one of their saints, Sara-la-Kali. They flowed into the town over a week. On the final Sunday, they formed a precession carrying a statue of their black skinned saint into the Mediterranean Sea. Arnfin claimed the gypsies gathered in camps every evening to hold flamenco guitar competitions. That sounded too good to pass up.

Winding down work, I quit my job in the lumber yard at the end of May and left the restaurant a few days later. My bank account had enough money in it to cover a few months' expenses. On the kibbutz in Israel, I would work eight hours a day for room and board. While at the Ulpan, Hebrew school took up four of those hours each morning leaving four hours to work in the fields.

I planned to hitchhike across France and Spain to Madrid, where I figured on staying for a while with Eleanor's family. Then I would hitch north again over the French border and through the marshes of the Camargue to meet Arnfin.

The youth hostel he told me about was in the festival town of Sainte-Marie de La Mer. Arnfin had shown me some pictures of this region filled with abandoned castles and tall grasslands. Some of the photos depicted wild horses running through marshes, their white manes silhouetted in aquamarine. The region looked magnificent. From La Camargue, I would hitchhike to Marseille for a day or two, then catch a Turkish boat to Tel Aviv. I already had my ticket. I had signed up for the kosher meals, an option highlighted near the top of the ticket order form. What kosher meals were, I had no idea. If they were featured in big bold letters, they must be very good.

CHAPTER FIVE
French Rhapsodies

The Road to Spain

Hitch hiking had served me well in Australia. Traveling the 1,500 kilometers from Dijon to Madrid would present no problem, or so I thought.

The first driver picked me up just outside of Dijon. A black Citroen DS pulled to the shoulder of the road. The car looked more like a badly designed boat than a well designed car. Considered a wealthy man's transportation, it had deep bucket seats and hydraulic suspension that created an exceptionally smooth ride. The driver reached over and opened the passenger door growling in slurred French, "If you are going toward Lyon, get in!"

The driver wore a dark suit with a pencil thin red tie pulled tight against his white collar. He turned his face, a grim rainbow of blue and red splotches, toward the road. Hesitantly, I climbed in. The interior reeked of wine and cigarettes.

His beady eyes glanced quickly sideways sizing me up as I settled into the cushiony seat. The car's plush cabin contrasted with the thick tension that filled the air. My thoughts of striking up a conversation vanished in the heavy silence. After a brief moment watching over his shoulder, he hit the gas. We darted into traffic.

The car jerked across the shoulder onto the country road, bolting forward like a rocket. Thrown back in my seat, blood rushed to my head as we roared down the highway weaving between trucks and cars. This guy used that deadly middle lane of the three lane highway like a matador. I peeked discretely over at the speedometer discovering to my horror that the needle was bouncing around close to one hundred and fifty kilometers per hour. Sweat dripped from my armpits. Barely dodging vans and trucks whose bumpers were at eye level, we narrowly avoided head-on collisions several times. Around curves, the car lifted to one side as I slid toward the passenger door struggling to stay in my seat.

This madman never said a word to me for two and a half hours. His hands turned red from gripping the wheel; his elbows locked stiffed-arm pushing his back into the seat. When he dropped me off on the outskirts of Lyon without saying goodbye, I felt very shaky. I doubted he would make it all the way to his destination. If he did, I felt sorry for those who awaited his wrath. Thanking God that I had not died in a fiery auto crash, I went into a nearby bistro for a beer and to wind down before continuing my trip. The atmosphere of the next ride changed completely. An amiable young student picked me up. She was headed to Montpellier not far from the Spanish border. She had one of those accents of the people in Southern France. A song-like blending of sentences, it was similar to the accent so familiar from my childhood back in Tennessee.

The sun shone bright that afternoon. She was wearing a short skirt that revealed generous sections of her shapely thighs and toned calves. Girls didn't usually pick up hitchhikers. For a moment, fantasy got the best of me as I wondered how I could convince her to take me with her on an exciting new adventure.

After a while, I realized that she was a sweet country girl with a generous heart and a friendly nature. I came around to seeing that by giving me a ride she was doing a good deed in helping a stranger. Her trusting disposition reminded me why I felt so comfortable in France. She talked about life in the south and her studies in sociology. When she dropped me off on the outskirts of Montpellier, I wished her a safe journey starting to feel more relaxed about hitchhiking, although a bit worried considering it was approaching five p.m. How far would I be able to travel before nightfall?

There was good reason to worry. It took a long time for another car to stop. The sun was fading. This next ride, a young couple heading south, took me across the Spanish border dropping me off north of Barcelona. It was already after dark when I stepped out of the car. The area where they left me was semi-rural. Not a hotel in sight. With almost no possibility of anyone stopping after nightfall, I searched around for a place to sleep.

A ways down the road, I came across a construction site with a few dozen homes in varying degrees of completion. I found one that was pretty far along. It had walls, windows and a roof installed, but no doors. This seemed like a perfect location to take shelter for the night. I worked my way into one of the back bedrooms, stretched out using my suitcase as a pillow and dozed off to sleep.

A blaring light jolted me abruptly from my slumber. As my eyes adjusted to the light, I was squinting into the barrels of two rifles. It took a minute before I could focus on the two men standing over me shouting something in Spanish. These men wore blue military-like uniforms and odd shaped caps that looked like poorly designed boats perched on their heads.

No need for a translator. From their gestures, I knew they wanted me to put my hands up. I slowly stood placing my hands on top of my head. I tried to communicate, "Me Americano… Je vais a Madrid… .Estudiante, Autostop…hitch hike.. Madrid… my amigos in Madrid." "Dormir… sleeping… no hotel" I stammered. Their rifles still fixed on me; they motioned for me to go out of the house. One of them picked up my suitcase.

We walked down a dirt road until we came to a village by the side of the highway. They took me inside a one-story concrete building. One of the men motioned for me to sit down before a metal desk. The other set my suitcase on the desk. He shuffled through my belongings while calmly exchanging words in Spanish with the officer behind the

154

desk. They did not appear to be either angry or concerned. Next, they marched me out onto a screened patio, motioned to a table signaling for me to sit. They left.

When they did not come back, I put my head down on the table and fell asleep. A bright sun woke me up some hours later. My suitcase stood abandoned in one corner of the porch. I looked around. Not a soul. I went into the office to check in with my captors. The office was as empty as the porch. I picked up my suitcase and walked out of the porch's unlocked screen door. I headed down the street to the highway; stuck my thumb in the morning breeze. Moments later, a man on his way to Barcelona picked me up.

Barcelona differed from any French city I had visited. Many of the structures were made of a clay-like substance or of stone. They lacked the decorative iron grill work, elaborately carved entrances, or black tiled roofs so prevalent in France.

The place had rawness to it. Spanish architecture shared the same heavy shuttered windows, old narrow cobblestone streets and wide avenues. Yet, the forms were stripped of any panache, more basic, centered on the functional. They had an organic quality.

The colors stayed closer to the earth. Streets lined with beige and brownstones separated by the occasional variety of dwellings painted in washed out blues and pale reds cut across the horizon. Lots of yellow and tan walls wove their way through the city. Even the outskirts of Barcelona were enshrouded in terracotta tones. It was as if structures had grown up out of the earth like giant tree stumps.

Life here moved at a different pace. I had arrived shortly after one in the afternoon. Everything was closed until four p.m. I would have to wait to buy food or supplies. I decided to continue on to Madrid. Walking to the edge of the nearest avenue that led to the highway, I stuck out my thumb.

The first ride took me through the suburbs of Barcelona to the main highway to Madrid. A half hour later, an old station wagon pulled over to give me a lift. Inside a man and his wife sat in the front seat. The back seat had been dropped down to make a long bed. Two small children stretched out in the back among bundles made from colorful fabrics. They all wore clothing embellished with bright green red and yellow bands. The whole family had jet black hair, dark skin and darker eyes. They looked poor. I crawled in the back between the kids and the bundles. We rolled down the road at a slow but steady pace while cars zoomed passed. I could only manage a few words in Spanish and didn't say much of anything. They laughed and talked with each other in warm voices giving me a good feeling about them.

Some of the passing drivers yelled angry words that sounded like insults as they passed, some even spit at our station wagon. When we stopped for gas, the attendant eyed us suspiciously the whole time. I saw an ugly side of Spanish behavior on this ride to Madrid. These Spaniards' attitude bothered me in the same way those "white only" bathrooms and "black only" water fountain signs had haunted me long after we moved north from Tennessee. I was a young boy and didn't really understand why they were there. Still, they didn't seem right. Like devils watching me from the shadows, their reflections surfaced from deep in my memory.

I felt comfortable traveling with this family. Nothing seemed to bother them as they talked and laughed along the road. We stopped once to picnic in a field and they shared their bread, olives, and smoked fish with me. Their children rolled around in the back playing a game with pieces of string tied to dowels. When they finally dropped

156

me off that night just outside of Madrid, I felt badly for the treatment dished out to them by those angry Spaniards. I was grateful to this generous family for the ride.

Stepping into the countryside, I checked around, a little more cautious this time, to see if anyone was watching me. I walked down a secluded street until coming to a field. I located a nice batch of tall grass near a tree and cleared a spot for myself. It was a warm night. Laying my suitcase on the ground, I took a final look about to make sure no one was in sight and settled in for the night.

Waking with the sun, my body felt a bit grungy but rested. I got an early start. The man who picked me up on his way to work in Madrid knew precisely where the US base was located. He gave me the impression that it was a well known landmark in the region. As he dropped me off at a bus terminal along his route, he pointed out exactly which bus I should take. The bus driver also seemed to understand what my destination would be just by looking at me. He signaled me to take the seat behind him.

Torrejon, A Land of Oz

Stepping off the bus, I understood why so many locals knew of this place. An endless expanse of chain link and barbed wire stretched across the horizon. Large U.S. flags flapped overhead in a light breeze. The two guards at the gate were tall and fair skinned looking like they had just walked off a Hollywood set. Their voices twanged in that Yankee squeal which, not so long ago, I would not even have noticed. Treating me like an expected cousin, they issued me a visitor permit and gave me directions to Eleanor's house. I passed through the fencing and turned a hundred yards beyond the guard station to follow a winding road that led away from the central compound.

Advancing deeper into the garrison felt like strolling down the Yellow Brick Road. All the ancient Mediterranean buildings and cobblestone roads vanished. In their place, wide streets covered in blacktop with white dashed lines down the middle meandered ahead. Cement sidewalks wound along the edges of neatly mowed grass lawns. One story wood framed houses, all painted yellow, with two car garages filled the landscape. The wide driveways exposed basketball hoops centered over the garage doors. Bicycles and tricycles huddled next to the railings of porches. Children's blue plastic swimming pools and green swing sets stood haphazardly about the back yards.

Buicks, Fords and Chevrolets parked in the driveways looked like dinosaurs, even bigger than I had remembered. The leased Peugeot which had appeared huge to me in Dijon was modest by comparison. Walking these few hundred yards, I had traveled five thousand cultural miles back to an American suburb. By some architectural feat of wizardry, I had stepped into Dorothy's Kansas.
Eleanor lived in one of these homes in the center of the block. She met me at the door and introduced me to Louise, her mother. Louise ushered me to a bedroom that I was to share with one of Eleanor's younger brothers,

The entire inside of their home unfolded before me like the pages of a storybook in which I knew all the characters by name. The living room felt as America as the outside of the house. Danish modern furniture, earth tone carpeting, big pane glass windows filled the modestly sized room. The kitchen's tiled countertops, the chrome table with its red marbled Formica surface and the vinyl padded metal chairs, every familiar detail brought the past to life. Louise directed me through the kitchen to the refrigerator, she opened its door. The refrigerator bulged with foods I had not seen in a few years. Baloney and white bread, milk in waxed paper half gallons, a red squeeze bottle of ketchup sat beside a bright yellow tub of creamy mustard.

Velveeta cheese lay behind a clear plastic flip-open door right next to the rectangular sticks of butter. Dill pickles floated in a half filled jar on the door rack across from the Iceberg lettuce resting in a transparent plastic vegetable drawer.

Then she made a familiar offer, one that erased two years of globe trotting with a single declaration. "Whenever you get hungry, just help yourself to whatever you want." Suddenly, I was home again.

Eleanor worked at the PX along with her younger brother. Her older brother was attending school in another part of Spain for the summer. This left me with a lot of free time to wander around the base and relax. However, I soon discovered that many areas on the base were either restricted access or completely off limits. My domain became the housing track, the PX and the swimming pool.

The first couple of days I hung out with Eleanor in the evenings talking about Dijon or watching American TV. It was so relaxing to be "home" that I didn't even want to visit Madrid. I preferred hanging around the PX, the base's supermarket that Eleanor's father managed. This store was another warehouse of American culture. The inside looked exactly like supermarkets back in California, full of familiar products.

In the late mornings, my most frequented haunt became the base swimming pool. There, groups of sexy young women lay on the warm pavement in bikinis that revealed lots of flesh while their soldier husbands marched all over the base, missing its most pleasing spectacle. I never got up enough nerve to talk to any of these lovely creatures as I kept imagining their husbands not far off with loaded guns. The ladies gradually took on a dreamlike quality, mermaids sunbathing in a pond. This artificial home town lulled me into a mild comma. Every morning the sun was

159

bright and the air mild and dry. Each day faded into the next as my stomach stretched to the limit with comfortable bland foods. My senses became duller and duller.
In fact, the whole stay with Eleanor was like a mirage.

How could this be and why? On a thousand acres of land, the US Air Force had created an American theme park just outside of Spain's largest city. Cozy and confusing, this wonderland caught me by surprise. It enchanted me those first few days. But, after about a week, the illusion started to grow burdensome. I began, inexplicably, to feel troubled and restless.

I started to pass the afternoons sitting by myself on the curb for long periods of time watching the occasional jeep roll by much as I had done when we first moved to Riverside. My mind drifted back to dark thoughts, anger, defeating memories of my high school rage. Ashes from the pyre of my adolescence smoldered on in a slow burn. I realized that I was not ready to return to the States. I thanked Eleanor and her family for their generous reception and headed north to seek out the gypsies.

Saint Marie de La Mer

The trip north was quick and uneventful until I caught the last ride with a young French couple headed to the festival and we entered *La Camargue*. Marshlands filled with tall grass lined the two lane road in deep shades of green as we crossed the region. Every now and then, crumbling stone structures rose up from the moor, meager remains of what must have once been medieval castles. Only an occasional tree appeared in the mired countryside. As we got closer to the town, the smell of salt and sea breezes filled the air. Sand began to build up along the shoulders of the road until grasslands turned into sandy knolls.
Cars pulling campers started to appear. Only a few at first scattered along the roadside. Then, they became more fre-

quent and began to form clusters on the sandy flatlands just before we entered the city. The Mediterranean filled the horizon as we rolled into the small village. Rows of white clay and sand colored houses cramped together along the road that converged onto a central square. A small church with a wide arching façade stood near the middle of town. A cluster of medieval buttresses pressed in, supporting the ancient building.

It did not take long to find the youth hostel where Arnfin had already checked in. This hole-in-the-wall dive was separated into the men's and women's quarters. To describe the dormitory as wooden bunks would have been generous. They were just flat wood slat decks stacked three high and held together with two by four cross beams. The room resembled those World War II pictures of the concentration camp barracks. Where one person's bed ended and the next person's began was left to the imagination. The island toilets with foot pads and a hole between them were something I had become accustomed to by now. However, the make-shift showers constructed from a long brass pipe with holes punched in clusters along its length did not look inviting.

I found Arnfin in one of the handful of cafés in the town. He was sitting his legs crossed, his foot bobbing against the empty chair next to him. His skinny arms, which covered most of the small round glass table, held a notepad between them. I figured Arnfin occupied about one and a half times the space allocated to the average local.

"*Chao mon vieux*," he greeted me. "Where you been? Two days here now and the crowds are growing. Tomorrow morning is the procession."
"Madrid, lost track of time, thought I was in California ….. Beautiful mermaids."

Arnfin looked excited, "Gypsies are showing up everywhere, their kids running around. I've been exploring the area. Found the church where the statue of Saint Sara is kept. A priest told me that the Romanian gypsies started this whole thing. Tonight should be interesting. You and I can go see what's happening. There's only a few tourists around." Arnfin spoke excellent English. His French was pretty good too. I admired those Nordic people when it came to languages. Then again, how many people in the world speak Danish?

It was already mid-afternoon as my stomach growled in protest. We stayed for a while in the café. I ordered a French *sandwich* from the glass display counter, one of those skinny baguettes sliced down the middle with paper thin pieces of ham and a narrow gruyere cheese lining, mostly bread. A pencil line of French mustard ran down the middle. Meager fare, but it tasted pretty good with a beer.

By late afternoon, we were ready to roam around and check out the town. There weren't many people on the streets. As we cut down one narrow passage to get closer to the beach, we saw three scrubby boys headed our way. They must have been twelve or fourteen years old wearing dirty jeans and what once must have been brightly colored shirts. Dark skinned with straight black hair sticking out here and there, they looked pretty rough. After coming within a few feet of each other in the narrow passageway, we all stopped. There was barely enough room to get past. Arnfin blared out his unfiltered thoughts. In that Nordic way, he got right to the point using clearly articulated French. "You boys carryin' knives? I heard that gypsies all carry knives."

"Don't listen to this fool, he's crazy. You don't have to answer that." I jumped in, hoping they spoke French.

162

For a long moment, they fixed us in their dark eyes, "Yaa, we got knives," the tallest of the bunch calmly replied, smiling wryly back at us. They did speak French. He gestured to the other boys who all nodded in agreement. A few of them reached into their pockets and pulled out black handled switch blades.

For a brief moment, we just stood there looking at each other, wondering. We were much bigger than they were, but they had the knives. They hesitated. Maybe we looked just as scary to them as they did to us. Nordic invaders. "Don't mind us. We're just students here to enjoy the festival," finally came out of my mouth.
"Where's the guitar music gonna be tonight? I love Flamenco. I read all about competition parties. Where should we go to see those?" Arnfin grinned forging ahead in blind determination.

At this remark, they all frowned. The tallest among them spoke, "Music's gonna be all around the camps. But you can't go. This is our festival. It's our music. It's between our families, not for outsiders." He said this without anger, like he was stating a fact he had heard his father tell foreigners many times. We got the point. Moving carefully forward, Arfin and I passed the boys leaving as much distance as possible between us and them, keeping a watchful eye as we turned onto the street.

By the time night finally did settle over the town, Arnfin had already shown me most of the highlights, which wasn't much. We ventured out of town towards the gypsy caravans in spite of the boys' admonishment.

You could hear the sound of guitars and haunting singing, like the howling of ghosts. We walked for a while along the main highway, and then turned south towards the beach. Here and there, embers from campfires drifted upward flickering in the night. To my surprise, Arnfin agreed that we did not want to abuse or disrupt the festivities. We wandered along a sandy bluff in the shadows a few hundred yards away from the sea, just behind the campfires. Beautiful apocalyptic sounds passed overhead riding on the wind and drifted out to sea. We found a patch of turf overlooking the Mediterranean, settled into the sand to share a bottle of Bordeaux.

We sat in silence watching the moonlight flicker across the sea. Sparkling rays bounced along the crests of waves weaving in and out of view. Flamenco rhythms accompanied their ebb and flow like dancers in a gypsy Fantasia. Late the next morning, I woke still feeling tired after a lousy night's sleep on those hard wooden slats. It had come as a surprise to me that people staying in this youth hostel were expected to bring sleeping bags. My suitcase, serving as a pillow, was the most comfortable aspect of my night. I should have just slept on the beach.

The streets were calm when Arnfin and I settled into our bistro chairs for some *café au lait* and croissants. By the time we finished breakfast, gypsies started showing up from all directions, gathering around the church square. By one o'clock, a pretty big crowd had built up and some men on white horses in white and red costumes appeared wearing wide brimmed sombreros. We joined the crowd as four gypsies exited the church. Pallbearers, each of the four men held a thick pole on his shoulder that extended from the four sides of a wooden platform. In the center of the platform sat a large statue dressed in white robes; a circular white halo perched on her head. The ornate statue rocked from side to side as they ambled forward. It was covered with glittering silver and gold braid work. The figure looked like a black Madonna. Men on horseback surrounded the sacred icon. Women in colorful outfits came up to touch the figure's gown before forming a precession in front and behind the pallbearers.

164

The procession moved slowly along the dirt road to the sea as women chanted. The horseman rode into the Mediterranean alongside the pallbearers who got wet up to their knees. After blessings and prayers, the procession returned to the church. They brought the statue inside and continued the festival. The ceremony lasted less than two hours, but it was a kaleidoscopic affair. I was glad to have been there. Since everything in France closed on Sunday, I decided to leave that afternoon. It wasn't that far to Marseille and my ship sailed in two days. I did not want to miss it. I decided to bid farewell to Arnfin who planned to stay a bit longer before returning to Copenhagen. His notebook had filled with notes. I hitched a ride north and was picked up by a French couple.

A Flirtatious Journey

Marseille turned out to be a dirty port city. The best part of my stay there was the youth hostel. This modestly restored old castle sat on a hill overlooking the city. The place actually provided beds, sheets and a pillow. Showers and toilettes were clean and modern. I stayed at the hostel for my time in Marseille and I felt rested by the time my ship began boarding passengers.

Our mud white ferry boat pulled its hull away from the drab harbor mid-morning. The boat spanned a hundred plus meters, its four decks crammed with passengers. I had to walk down a narrow hallway into the belly of the ship to reach my cramped room. This economy berth was a windowless hole lit by a single bulb in a metal cage. The bunk, some five feet in length, forced me to sleep in a fetal position. What did I expect? It was cheap and the journey lasted less than a week.

The main dining hall was crammed with long metal tables bolted to the floor and sat at least a hundred people. It filled twice a day with a lackluster crowd. Those seated at the table around me looked like characters from another century. Wearing dark outfits and curly bangs, they often appeared stiff with serious expressions. They never talked to me or the handful of other people at our table who dressed normally. The rest of the hall filled with chatter. People appeared to be enjoying themselves. Maybe choosing kosher had not been such a good idea.

Waiters brought the meals out. Instead of fluffy French bread with that snap and crackle crust, they set out little trays of flat crackers, tasteless slabs vaguely reminiscent of cardboard. The boiled fish and unseasoned vegetable dishes offered little relief to the insipid nature of these meals. Occasionally, flasks of dark red juice were deposited in the center of the table. The stuff smelled earthy and the taste conjured up images of drinking blood. Meals for Dracula on a diet. It was too late for me to move from the kosher section. Besides, I was committed to new experiences, no matter how disagreeable.

The weather was nice, the sea calm. Walking back and forth along the main promenade or leaning against the railing surveying the Mediterranean filled the daylight hours. Watching people provided a good amount of entertainment. Most of the passengers were much older or much younger than me. A lot of families looked Germanic or Middle Eastern

There was one other person close to my age who grabbed my attention. I first spotted the young lady sitting alone at a table on the far side of the dining hall. Stuck with the fundamentalist crowd, there was no way I could approach her during those busy mealtimes.
She had fair skin and straight black hair that flowed down along the sides of her face, rolling over her shoulders. The fineness of that dark hair accentuated her long neckline.
For a young woman of average stature, she had long legs, a

166

long waist, everything about her was long. Yet, she was thin boned and delicate.

When she surfaced one afternoon leaning against the railing of the promenade, I slowed my pace to get a better look. As her emerald eyes surveyed the passing crowd, I thought I detected a slight turning up at the corners of her lips.
"What's so interesting?" I ventured in English, leaning along side her.

Her eyes sparkled as if to invite me to share a secret, "You see that lady sitting on the deck chair reading the blue and white book? See her little boy? He's untied both her shoes. She's so busy reading that she only shakes her foot to get rid of the nuisance as she feels him tugging. He's pulling the laces apart now. Pretty soon she's going to shake her foot and her shoe will go flying." She flashed me another smile.

I looked over and, sure enough, it would only be a matter of time before the shoe sailed off her foot. Showing her a quiet smile, I moved a little closer to the ship's handrail. She leaned back against the rail bringing her head closer to mine. I could smell the fragrance of freshly shampooed hair in the sea breeze. How could I be so lucky!
As the days drifted by, we formed our own little detective team of two in search of comic situations. We spent a lot of time together on deck studying the idiosyncratic behavior of our fellow travelers. When we weren't laughing over some odd mishap, we swapped stories about our lives.
Vera, that was her name, liked to talk in a soft voice while leaning close to me, almost touching.
Once, I let my arm drop so that my hand rested against the side of her thigh. Vera pulled her body away. The aroma of her hair grew faint and I felt a sting of guilt. Nevertheless, our bond of affectionate intimacy continued to grow.

167

We gradually learned more about each other. Vera came from Geneva, a place I had never been. She made it sound sophisticated and wealthy. Yet, Vera seemed unconcerned with the material world. She described her trip to Israel as something uplifting that her family encouraged. Vera's destination was a kibbutz called Shefayim. She had an uncle there and planned to spend a few months working to help the young nation of Israel develop. Near the end of our voyage, she invited me to go with her to Shefayim. Vera smelled so good when she snuggled close to me. The attraction I felt for her in those moments nestled against the ship's railing was dizzying: I would have followed her anywhere.

The ship docked under clear skies in the port of Tel Aviv. The water was pristine. The dock was clean and well maintained. I had never seen a port like this with no cargo ships anywhere in sight, 'no grey cranes with their heavy steel cables cut ting scars across this bright blue and white skyline.

Once ashore, the first question Customs asked was whether or not I was Jewish. When the agent learned I was not, he reached below his counter changing to a different stamp and ink pad of a different color. He returned my passport folded open to the page which had writing that looked like a row of twisted flames in purple ink. Appearing smug in his confidence that I could not read the writing, this bureaucrat felt the need to explain to me in a loud voice that I would not be allowed to work for money during my stay in Israel. As he studied me coldly, I stared back at him with my best dumb dog look. The thought, *I will find a way to earn money here* flashed irreverently across my mind.

The Land of Milk and Honey
Vera and I caught a bus that followed the Coast north to Shefayim. It was a pleasant ride over palm-lined roads that

skirted a continuous stretch of sandy beaches. The sand was almost white. When we arrived at Shefayim late that morning, Vera talked to the man who met our bus. I grabbed my suitcase without hesitation. I already knew Vera would be irresistible in convincing him to let me stay. Single men and women resided in separate quarters on the kibbutz. The men's lodgings were wooden cabins that housed four. The women's section could be seen a few hundred yards away. Like a well organized campsite, two collective showers and bath houses located in the middle of the cabins served both complexes.

I shared my assigned cabin with an Indian and a North African. I quickly became friends with Mushin, the young man from Delhi. We may have seemed an odd pair to some people as I was so tall while Mushin was short with a slight build. Yet, I treated him with a great deal of respect. I had a long history of befriending shorter boys.
My best friend in high school, Mike, was short. He could go places and spend time with people unnoticed, something I could rarely do. Mike was craftier with a lot more courage than most people thought. He and I crashed parties together, got into sports events free. With Mike's inside information, we even tracked down one of the meanest bullies on the football team at a party one night and siphoned all the gas out of his truck. We drove all over town on that gas.

Mushin didn't get a lot of respect on the kibbutz. I suspected that I wasn't the only one who didn't know there were Jews in India. Shefayim's population looked a mix of German and Russian. Ironically, I resembled an Israeli more than Mushin. He told me about Delhi, where his family lived a meager life, and how he had come to Israel looking for a better one. Mushin was determined to make good here. I felt sure he would succeed.

169

The second day, I got my work assignment in the newly planted orchards as an assistant to an older man, a long-time resident. Our job, an eight hour shift, was to spray the fields with DDT to prevent infestations. They gave us big copper tanks to strap on our backs. Black rubber hoses extended down from a spout on the side of the tank to a spray nozzle attached to the end of the hose. We walked up and down the rows spraying plants near their base.

Even though it got hot during the day, I wore long socks, jeans and tennis shoes. My partner wore sandals on his bare feet, his legs exposed below the hem of his khaki shorts. As our paths crossed at the end of rows, I noticed big red and purple scabs all over his lower legs, especially near the ankles. This had to be strong poison we were putting down. I exercised a lot of caution to avoid getting any of the stuff on my body.

The best part of the job was mid-day break when we returned to the kibbutz for lunch. We ate lots of raw vegetables in salads. Only small portions of meat were served but lots of fruit placed on the tables finished the meal. Spices were almost never used. These weren't mouth watering meals. Yet within a few days, I began to feel great after eating this way, light and full of energy. I never went hungry or felt stuffed.

One evening a few days later, the long awaited chance came for Vera and me to slip away. After dinner, we made our way out to a secluded spot on the beach and watched the sun set. The day drifted into a balmy summer night. With no one in sight, the two of us were at last completely alone. Vera was wearing a tight fitting one piece bathing suit. She looked terrific.

After sitting there for a long while, I got up the nerve to kiss her. During the first kiss we barely touched lips. I noticed that Vera's expression became tender when our eyes met during the next kiss which lingered on. For the next kiss she closed her eyes and gently pulled me down with her on the warm sand. We pressed close, side by side, kissing gently. We kissed and kissed and kissed. Vera lay motionless never opening her eyes. I got up more nerve and slid my hand along her leg until it reached the edge of her bathing suit. The tight elastic band formed a tough barrier. I sensed that I was going to have trouble getting under the elastic without a lot more force. My hand began to slide along the smooth edge of her suit. Just as I approached the upper most portion of her inner thigh, my hand stopped its forward journey.

As we kissed, I continued to explore her exposed legs and arms. I rubbed her back. Vera relaxed her muscles, becoming unusually docile. Yet, every time my hands met the boundary of that bathing suit, I couldn't bring myself to move forward into more intimate territory. Each new approach grew weaker as my confidence began to vanish. That slight rejection on the ship came to mind, my sense of guilt grew. I couldn't shake the odd thought that my mother would not approve of any perverse behavior with this fine young lady. Vera gave me no indication one way or the other. I could tell she liked the kissing and hoped she wanted more. If only she would give me a clue. Pull me closer, squirm a little, moan a little, anything.

She lay passive, waiting. Vera was so smart, very sharp witted. She must have a plan. Maybe I was being too aggressive. Maybe I should back off to gain her respect. Next time she would be more willing, more enthusiastic. "Always be a gentleman," my mother's ghost whispered in the back of my mind. My mother was a smart woman. Surely, she would admire my gallantry.
I sat up offering Vera my hand like a gentleman. "We should probably go back," I heard myself say in a mousy voice. Neither of us talked as we walked back to the complex. I felt really frustrated, stupid.

171

The next day, I returned to working in the fields with a heavy heart. I didn't like this job and continued to steer clear of the nasty smelling liquid that splashed against the ground. I kept wearing high top tennis shoes in the heat of the day.

With separate lodging and working for hours in the fields, I rarely had a chance to see Vera after that evening on the beach. In the days that followed, she and I only spoke briefly to each other across the dining hall. Our conversations became less intimate and she began to disappear after evening meals. I had failed to meet the challenge. I couldn't believe my mother's old fashioned ideas influenced me over such a great distance and after so long. I believed that my mother, with her old fashioned morals, would never have allowed herself to be caught locked in those intensely amorous clutches. Had I gone mad?

One afternoon when I got home from the fields, Mushin came over to my bed. He looked troubled. "I don't like to tell you this Richard. I saw your friend Vera last night. She was holding hands with one of the Sabras walking towards the beach. They did a lot of sweet smiling. I didn't want to tell you but, you must watch out for that girl."
Mushin's words made me even angrier with myself. That could have been me walking out to the beach for Round Two of some serious passion. What was I thinking? It stung to realize what a dummy I had been. That Puritan upbringing tormented me at the most inconvenient times. How could I have behaved like such a coward?

My anger extended to the crummy job in the orchards. All night I kept dreaming about big red and purple scabs circling overhead. I went out to the bath house and took a second shower. One thought began to dominate all the others, *to hell with this place.*

Early the next morning, I quietly told Mushin goodbye. After breakfast, I snuck back to my cabin, avoiding the truck that brought us to the fields, and shoved my belongings into my bag. I walked to the road and stuck out my thumb. It really didn't matter where I went as long as it was away from here. I headed north toward Haifa.

Dawn at the Ulpan

Sitting on the edge of my bunk in the youth hostel in Haifa, my thoughts kept drifting back to Vera and the way I left. Some horrid Puritan demon had possessed me that night. I felt like I had been reduced to a shy, fearful boy. Yet, perhaps I hadn't lost her to indecisiveness that night on the beach. Maybe, Vera had already moved on in her mind; maybe she wanted to get involved with people from Israel, immerse herself in the life and culture. I could understand if she did. Maybe she just wasn't that interested in me. Vera popped up constantly in my thoughts. I didn't want to think about her anymore. Why did I care?

What bothered me also was the way I had slipped away from Shefayim. Leaving had become a way of life for me. I wondered whether I was truly an adventurer searching to discover the wonders of this world or just running away from my past. What was I looking for? At times, it felt more like something was chasing me. Whatever pursued me, I felt caught in Haifa as I sat on the bed looking across the empty room. There was no getting away from that sad face I saw in the mirror.

These troubled thoughts intermingled with wanderings around Haifa. I discovered a wonderful falafel stand near a bus stop, beautiful beaches with spectacular sunsets. That orange ball burnt out in a fiery rainbow of reds and yellows, then rolled into the sea bringing obscurity.
In the face of such a magnificent spectacle, I finally found some inner peace. If the entire earth went dark every even-

173

ing only to be reborn at daybreak, it didn't really matter whether I was running from or looking for something. Vera didn't matter; I didn't matter. We were all just in this world, tiny specks behaving exactly the way we were designed, like the sun sinking into the sea.

Before leaving the hostel, I leaned against the door and took a final survey of the room. There were no pictures on the wall. The white sheets stretched tight over a small mattress resting on the grey steel box springs would soon be changed. Another unknown soul would sleep here, wiping out any trace of my existence. It was time to step away from the ghosts of Shefayim. I left for my original destination, the Ulpan at Alomin. I would arrive a few days ahead of the start of classes.

Alomin had a lot of charm. Set in an oak tree grove, it was less arid in this region of the country. The complex was laid out in much the same way as Shefayim. Except the quarters for girls and boys were closer together, separated only by the small schoolhouse. The whole school campus set apart from the rest of the kibbutz by a few hundred yards. Until classes started, they sent me out to the fields to pick fruit.

Over the next few days, a lot of kids from New York City began moving into the cabins. Some of the girls were pretty cute. These young people spoke rapidly in dry cutting tones. Their voices crackled with arrogance like city folks. I felt intimidated and stayed to myself, didn't talk much. The first day of class we got our textbook. It was a grey book with no pictures. A thick hardcover, its pages were filled with many tables and lists of words in Hebrew script, English definitions next to them. My little French book back in Sydney had more pictures and smiling stick figures. The teacher barked at us in a stern confident voice. Yet, he came across as being more protective than hostile. Going to Hebrew school reminded me a bit of those kosher meals. Boring and tasteless, it didn't look like school held out much promise of being enjoyable. But, I intended to try.

A few of the other young people in the class seemed as though they had come to the wrong place. Before long, we found each other. There was another dark skinned Indian. The Indian guy and I became friends much as with Mushin. His slow steady speech and gentle manner made him easy to like. One girl wore thigh-high leather boots and knitted skirts to evening meals. The girl captured my full attention the moment she spoke. She had an Australian accent.

Dawn was her name. Every time she smiled, I felt like the sun had come up to shine on me. This young lady had milky smooth skin. Her face was round and warm. It filled with kindness. Her vagabond-swank style of dress reminded me of the crowd at the Brass Lantern, that Beatnik pub near Sydney harbor.
It turned out that Dawn knew the place well, had hung out there with her former husband. She was one of the in-crowd back in Sydney. Dawn even thought she knew Sonia. I had no desire to find out just how well she knew Sonia.

Dawn reminded me of the best qualities of the Australians. She loved adventure, wasn't afraid to strike out on her own. She had come to Alomin to explore life in Israel and test her ability to learn Hebrew, much like myself.

Dawn had that uniquely Australian sense of humor. It was a subtle kind that snuck into the conversation and hung in the air until somebody got it or just let it rest. Even though she was at Alomin on her own, she knew other Australians bumming around Israel. She had traveled to Greece and Turkey with her husband before they split up.

Being around Dawn didn't involve quick-witted banter and knowing looks. It was just easy like sitting on the front porch back in Ohio, rolling with the flow and letting the world move along. We spent our free hours together not doing much or saying much, all the while feeling good.

But those Hebrew classes were painful. We students spent long hours spitting out words and gargling up strange sounds. We sacrificed our evenings reading lists over and over to each other, only to forget it all by daybreak. It was the only time I can remember enjoying working in the fields more than going to school.

One night, I went over to visit Dawn in her cabin. She was bunking with this real pretty girl from New York. By pretty, I mean she had a slim waist, flat tummy, a round behind and firm bulging breasts. Her legs tapered to the ankle. The reason I know such intimate details is because when I walked in the room, this young Aphrodite was walking around the little cabin wearing only a skimpy black bra and matching lacey panties.
She didn't fuss or cover up upon my arrival. No, she just kept on walking around the room like everything was normal. It was a thoroughly enjoyable sight and I was not about to complain. Unfortunately, it didn't take long for

Dawn to get fired up about my misdirected attention.
"What are you doing in your underwear with a boy in the room? Get some clothes on right now," Dawn growled at the girl.
"What for? It's hot and Richard doesn't mind, do you, Rich? She replied with that cool city attitude.
"No really, I don't mind at all," I replied in a polite tone trying to look innocent. That's when Dawn chased me out and got that girl dressed before I could come back in.

The next night, I strolled into Dawn's cabin to find her alone on the bed. The roommate was gone and a thin scarf

176

lay over the lampshade giving off a seductive orange glow. I sat next to Dawn on the bed. We began to kiss. She had warm soft lips that melted against mine as we fell back on the bed. In no time, we were naked dissolving into each other as her flesh cradled me like God's softest pillow. I disappeared into our passion, no longer able to tell where I ended and Dawn began. I felt myself float away on a cloud of contentment and fell asleep. Dawn had to wake me up and boot me out in order to make sure we would not get in any trouble.

Another week passed, before Dawn and I decided we wanted to live together. I asked our teacher if we could move into one of the couple's cottages. He said that was out of the question. This was a school for young people to learn, not a house of ill repute.

Pounding away at Hebrew wore on me. Memorizing lists of words in no way resembled the enthusiastic struggle to find those phrases that would allow me to purchase a freshly baked pastry in a French boulangerie. None of the New Yorkers attempted to speak Hebrew with each other after class. The Sabras on the kibbutz never came to talk to us. The only contact we had with them was in the fields where conversation was not encouraged.

I decided that the remainder of my stay in Israel should be dedicated to enjoying the summer. My original fantasy, based on my experiences in France, of learning Hebrew through assimilation into the culture proved unrealistic, not achievable in just a few months. Dawn wasn't doing much better learning the language. Her motivation puttered along at about the same low level as my own.
She came up with a solution that appealed to me on more than one level. Dawn knew of a place in Israel called Eilat. It was at the southern most tip of the country across from the Bay of Aqaba, a Jordanian port where Lawrence of Arabia once stayed. Eilat sounded like another drab indus-

177

trial port and mining town. At the apex of the Red Sea, trade routes from there led south to the Indian Ocean and east to Asia. Friends had told her the seawater in Eilat was so salty that your body would float high on its surface.

Some of her Australian friends had gone there staying for free in tents on the beach. Best of all, from my point of view, was the reason they gave for going to Eilat. The Timna Copper Mines just north of town paid a modest wage to foreign workers. They always needed people, paid in cash at the end of the work day and their workers did not have to be Jewish. How could I pass up such an opportunity for money? What better way to defy that Israeli customs officer's arrogant command?

Eilat's Poisoned Dogs
We caught a bus south across the Negev, on a barren stretch of desert road that terminated at the station in Eilat. This town was a bleak mining camp with a small port and lots of prefabricated buildings. One big exception was a ten story hotel on the northern most tip of the seashore. Its beach front was bounded by a tall chain link fence that extended a hundred feet into the Red Sea. Down the beach, outside the hotel fence, fifty or so canvas tents formed a make-shift village. They were lined up in a row close to the bus station. Dawn found some Australians who were leaving and set us up with their two-person tent in the middle of the encampment.

The bus station locked its toilets and the hotel blocked all access to its facilities. The only other structure remaining on the beach was an abandoned building, probably a restaurant at one time, near the tents. All the windows and doors were long gone. There was no roof and the inside offered no comfort and little shelter, just a large slab floor. The inhabitants of the tents used it as the communal toilette. Bring your own paper and watch where you stepped

178

were the only two rules. As for baths, there were none. A plunge in the Red Sea had to pass for taking a bath. It was true what they said about the sea; my body floated half way out of the water. I quickly understood that the Red Sea provided a lousy bath when I tried to shake my body free of all that salt, especially the chunks in my hair.

Dawn and I settled in quickly. It didn't take long to get a job at the Timna Mining Co. which the locals called Solomon's Mines. The mine was located twenty five kilometers north of Eilat with free bus runs daily to and from the horseshoe-shaped valley where the main facility was located. Its strip mining operation produced copper cement brought down to the processing plant by large ramped shoots that pressed against the red cliffs.

The job they gave me sent me climbing up and down those conveyor ramps that shuttled ore from the digs to the processing plant. A lot of hours in the desert sun browned my skin. No one worked with me, affording me the time to dream and scheme about the future. Cleaning pebbles, sand and other debris from the rollers was boring but pretty easy work. Very little dust floated in the air to bother me as I worked on the ramps. They were shut down for maintenance. My supervisor was a friendly, soft spoken Pakistani named Zamir. He had taken an interest in me and gave me one of the better jobs at the site. The rest of his crew was also Pakistani and showed him an unusually high level of respect.

Dawn found part time work at a local café waiting tables for cash in the evenings. The strict Israeli rules did not seem to apply in the lawless atmosphere of this end-of-the-road mining town. Walking to the company bus in the mornings, I would pass dead dogs lying in drainage ditches along the dirt alleys. They showed signs of having been poisoned with their bodies swollen into oversized footballs. Their legs were sticking up like rotting masts stiffly

179

defying the sandy gusts of hot wind that swept between the buildings. They lay in the same position for days as no one seemed to care or even notice.

The tent people kept to themselves a lot of the time. Most were only there to work at the Timna Mining Co. They behaved peacefully towards each other and occasionally gathered to chat in the evenings. Too tattered and worn to match my image of Beatniks, they struck me more as lost souls, young vagabonds. Abandoned metal platforms like the one in front of our tent served as benches used by the camp inhabitants to sit and talk in the evenings.
Several Australians and English drifters populated the tents. One night after a particularly nice sunset watching the lights flicker in the Arab town of Aqaba just across the bay, I sat on the bench waiting for Dawn to arrive with food from the diner. It felt like I was sitting at the edge of the world. Suddenly, an Englishman plopped down beside me from out of nowhere. He launched into a long monolog.

"Time's movin' fast. I been on the run for days now. Man on the run, that's me. They split the rock, shattered it into red veins flyin' through the air. Night lights closing down. Agents almost got me in Haifa, but I jumped a bus south. Liverpool's far away. I'd get there quick if I had to. Nothin' but trouble Liverpool. That bitch owes me. Cross the road if you see the key maker comin' there's a mute fool in those rocks above the bay. Pretends dumb, but talks to me. He ain't no fool. I know it, you know it. Speaks fire water.....Bobbies lookin' for him, too...they won't leave him alone......"

He rambled on like this for a half hour. I couldn't get in a word, didn't really want to anyway. Most of his steady stream of words made no sense. Yet, some things he said had some truth to them. An old mute did live in a cave two hills from town. The old man had lost part of his throat in

180

World War II. He showed up on the odd evening walking along the beach or among the tents. Incomprehensible hissing sounds gurgled out when he struggled to speak. He communicated by gesturing with his arms and hands. People in the tents called this hapless soul "The Caretaker of Aqaba Bay." I would have liked to learn more about this outcast, but my English companion kept up the incessant talk, constantly changing subjects. He couldn't stop fidgeting, causing the entire bench to rock.

His hands shook the whole time. I began to hope he would leave soon. Suddenly, in the middle of a sentence, he got up and walked off down the beach. Without looking back, he disappeared into the blackness until only the sound of waves hitting the shore remained.

The next morning word circulated around the camp that some English guy had died of an overdose of amphetamines the night before, just a few hundred yards from our tent. People were scurrying over to the bus station to take a look at the body before they hauled it away. I didn't move. An eerie feeling ran down my spine. I was probably the last person on this earth to hear his voice before this drifter dropped dead that night. It was the third time since I had left California that death had strolled across my path.

A little over three weeks had passed since I had signed on at the mines. I took lunch with Zamir and the crew on weekdays. We got pretty friendly. Zamir kept offering to let Dawn and me stay at his place for free. I didn't want to impose on my boss, but hadn't had a proper shower in so long that my hair was getting stiff. I finally gave in.

The following Saturday, Dawn and I grabbed our stuff and hiked up the hill to the cinderblock fourplex where Zamir lived. As soon as we walked through the door, a bad feeling came over me. The place was too empty, no pictures, no carpet, and no furniture. What looked like a rectangular coffee table occupied the center of the living room, except its legs were so short the table stood only a few inches above the floor. Three Pakistanis whom I had never seen before were sitting on cushions against the wall. They didn't even look up as we arrived. Zamir showed us into the only bedroom and pointed to the adjacent bathroom. "Why don't you and Dawn get cleaned up, then you can relax."

Dawn and I took a shower together. It felt really good to get all that dirt and salt out of my long hair. I hadn't had a haircut since leaving Dijon months earlier. I dressed and stepped out of the bathroom. Dawn followed wrapped in a towel. To my surprise, we entered to find Zamir standing in one corner. The bedroom door was closed. It appeared to be locked, leaving the three of us trapped in the cramped room.

Zamir waited for us to clear the bathroom door, his body bent slightly forward, face strained, his eyes glared at me. Although he spoke in that familiar slow steady manner, his voice had become menacing. Walking over to a night table, he opened a drawer and grabbed the jewel studded handle of an exotic looking knife.
"You see this knife? It is an ancient Turkish warrior's weapon." As he moved a little closer to us, he slowly pulled the knife from its metal sheath turning it cautiously in his right hand. The dagger was about nine inches long and three inches wide at the base. Its blade swept to a point like the horn of a rhinoceros. "There's something very special about this knife. Look at the tip. That brown streak, you see that? It's a secret poisonous mix. When it comes in contact with human blood, the victim is paralyzed for several hours. Even though the person is still conscious he can't move......."

Zamir was cut off by a pounding at the door. He reluctantly moved across the room. The loud voice of one of the

182

Pakistani men rattled the door. He continued shouting anxiously in some Arab language. Looking irritated, Zamir unlocked the door, opened it slightly and let the man stick his head in. The Arab, whom I recognized from the living room earlier, briefly took in the scene and looked a little surprised. He then focused on Zamir with a clear sense of urgency. They had a heated exchange and Zamir turned to us. His voice once again sounded cordial and friendly, "An urgent matter requires my immediate attention. Please make yourselves comfortable. Stretch out on the bed; take a nap. I'll return shortly."

We waited in the bedroom listening until all the commotion on the other side of the door had subsided. I opened the door and looked into the living room. Everyone was gone. I could hardly believe that they had left us all alone. How dumb did Zamir think I was? "Get dressed and grab your stuff. We're getting the hell out of here."
Dawn and I returned to the beach and our cozy little tent. Still, I spent a fitful night tossing and turning wondering if Zamir would show up at the camp. The next morning when I arrived at the company bus to go to the mines, the driver told me to step off the bus. He informed me that I no longer worked for the Timna Mining Co.

I walked back toward the beach, stopping at a small kiosk to buy coffee and rolls for a surprise breakfast with Dawn. As I turned toward the tents, one of the Pakistanis from our crew came over. "Listen to me carefully, Richard. Zamir's looking for you. You insulted him by leaving his apartment yesterday. Don't you know that he's a powerful heroin merchant in this town? If you're wise, you'll take your woman and leave Eilat before Zamir finds you." He looked around as if to make sure none of the other Pakistanis were in sight and scurried off toward the company bus without looking back.

No more encouragement was necessary to convince me of
the accuracy of his message. Dawn and I had our breakfast,
packed our things and went out to the main road. We
hitched north toward civilization.
Things weren't that bad. We both had saved up some money while in Eilat and were really clean for the first time in
weeks.

Dawn came through for us again. In the course of her casual conversations with people in the campsite, she had
learned of a kibbutz near the eastern boarder of Israel
where visitors only had to work half a day. The short
workday had something to do with gunfire in the area. We
headed for Ein Gev on the northeastern shores of the Sea
of Galilee.

Shelter Between the Palms
On the trip north, we kept getting rides from men traveling
alone. Maybe it was because of my long disheveled hair
and Dawn's vaguely hipster appearance, but the men all
asked the same question. About half way into our trip, they
would ask me. "Can I sleep with your girlfriend?"
Inside, I felt really angry with these backward Israeli oafs.
The first time it happened, I answered with an emphatic
"No." The second time, I started letting them know how it
felt. "Show me a picture of your wife or girlfriend you
want me to sleep with and I will think it over." That generally shut them up or at least forced a more reasonable conversation. Fortunately for me, none of them had a woman
to offer. I decided that when I got back to Dijon, I would
cut my hair.

Dawn wanted to see Jerusalem. We climbed up to the top
of this mountain where The Holocaust Museum was located. After reading a bronze plaque that described some of
the exhibits, including lampshades made from human skin,
I decided to wait outside. Other visitors told me that gun-

184

fire occasionally came from the Arab side of the city hitting this very location. The Jews weren't getting any relief even after centuries of persecution.

Of course, the Palestinian anger was understandable, but I couldn't figure out why all those so called "civilized" people hated the Jews so much and for so long. Some primeval hatred lurked inside waiting for those bitter moments to surface again and again. This museum was a testament to the vicious and despicable behavior exhibited by intolerant people through the centuries. This horror living in the shadows of our nature seemed overwhelming and inescapable. The place made me depressed. It made me ashamed to be alive.

The next day, Dawn wanted to see Nazareth. At least it was on the way. She was such a tourist, not at all hip according to my understanding of the Beatnik code. On the road to Nazareth, we were picked up by a truckload of Palestinians in white robes. We climbed in the back of the pick-up with about six guys.

After my experiences with Zamir and the Israeli farmers, I distrusted groups of men. I pulled out a pocket knife and began cleaning my fingernails with its longest blade while casting suspicious looks in their direction. One of them tapped on the cab window. Words were exchanged with the driver in Arabic. They kicked us off the truck. We had to hitch another ride. I felt foolish; it didn't seem that I needed to be so distrustful. My behavior had done little to improve relations with the Palestinians.

Nazareth's old city was really old. The clay church where Jesus preached felt sacred, magical and ghostly. We moved on to Hittim and visited the lake shore, waters on which Jesus was reported to have walked. I stuck my foot in. It didn't look possible to me to walk on that water. I struggled to believe that the water had softened up much during the two thousand year interim.

In the summer of 1965, Israel was an oddly shaped nation with no-man's lands scattered along the fringes of the country. Many Palestinians were trapped in refugee camps just outside its borders, especially in Jordan. These people wanted their homes back. They vented anger by shooting at Israelis and were particularly active in the disputed regions. One of these regions was along the eastern shores of the Sea of Galilee.

Israel held a narrow strip of land skirting either side of the eastern shore, two thin fingers that didn't quite touch. The gap between them was no man's land. From the rolling hills that overlooked the shoreline, Arabs used rifles to fire at the nearby kibbutzim and Israeli orchards.

Ein Gev sat at the northern most extremity of one of these fingers of land. A bus from Tiberius shuttled travelers around the lake to the very border of Israel. Dawn and I hopped on the bus just as daylight was thinning into darkness. By the time we traveled around the base of the Sea of Galilee, night had fallen.

As we swung north, the bus driver turned off the headlights. He made an announcement over a scratchy intercom in Hebrew. Unable to understand, I walked up to the front and asked in English why the lights were off.

"We're entering the zone where Palestinians once used our buses' headlights to guide their rifles on target."

"How can you drive in the dark?"

"There are reflectors along the road that shine in the moonlight. They guide the bus. Don't worry; I do this all the time. I've never run into anything and I've never taken a bullet. The Palestinians are lousy shots."

The driver was right. We did not drive off the road and I didn't hear any gunfire. Still, it made for an exciting ride. Ein Gev was a small place right on the lakeshore in a palm grove. The sparse population of the kibbutz added to the unexpected, even surprising, serenity of the place. The man in charge gave us a cozy little cabin made of cinder block right on the lake which presented a charming view of the sea from our window.

In Jerusalem, Dawn had managed to pick up a ticket on the same boat I was taking back to France. We sailed in three weeks. This would be our last stop in Israel and a chance to relax half the day on the sandy shore in the kibbutz complex.

When I learned the foreman in charge of work assignments on the kibbutz wanted me to work in the banana fields, my first reaction was fear. I had heard that snakes lived in the clusters of bananas on the trees. I didn't like the idea of a snake crawling out onto my shoulders. As it turned out, my job was to water the fields. I had to move long aluminum watering lines up and down the fields each day. This required walking across open patches of grass between the trees to rotate the pipes. I preferred taking my chances with the gunfire to facing the snakes.

Throughout the three weeks in Ein Gev there was constant gunfire, especially in the evenings. Yet, no one ever shot at me. The hills on the Jordanian side of the border rolled gently up slopes covered only with short dry grass. Anyone close enough to take a shot at me would have been readily visible and the banana trees provided plenty of places to hide. I never spotted a soul on those slopes. I checked every time before crossing the field.

One night, returning from the orchards, I found a lock of Dawn's hair on the writing table tied with a blue ribbon, her gift to me. I built a little shrine of palm leaves, gathered them around the base of a tin can which I placed up-side down. On the very top of the can, I placed the lock of hair. It stood there for a few days, a modest celebration of our natural affection for one another.

Our stay at Ein Gev proved to be a pleasant one overall. Dawn and I had the afternoons free to swim in the lake, read or just talk. I developed a taste for eating lots of raw vegetables and fruit. I felt great. My thoughts turned to Di-jon and the new school year.

Dawn began to knit me a sweater for the French winters. It was a kind gesture but, made me a little uncomfortable. We had talked about returning to France. She wanted to learn French and live there. This put me in an awkward situation, as I had reached a level of proficiency in the lan-guage that permitted me to speak only French while living in Dijon. As she knitted away, Dawn claimed she under-stood that we may not stay together after the end of the summer and accepted our possible separation.
Still, for the first time in my life, I had spent more than a few days with the same girl. Dawn shared my curiosity about the world. She was kind, loving and tolerant. Life on the road with her had been easy, even helpful, leaving me grateful for her company. Did I actually have a girlfriend? Being alone and moving on had always been fundamental for me. This was different.

For the first time, I felt guilty about what might happen when we got back to France. Dawn sensed my discomfort and claimed she had decided to study at Grenoble, a French town at the foothills of the Alps. We boarded the ship in Tel Aviv heading out across the Mediterranean, two souls suspended between worlds, held in an uneasy peace.

CHAPTER SIX
French Rhapsodies

Hallowed Ground

The regular food served during our return voyage aboard the same Turkish ship was not much better than those kosher meals on the way to Israel. Dawn and I were assigned a dinky metal cage of a cabin behind the galley. Every time we passed through the back of the kitchen, the galley crew gave us a bad time, mocking our appearance and making sexual overtures to Dawn. These young Turks were aggressive, grabbing at us in the narrow hallway. It took a few near fights before they finally backed off. When at last my feet touched French soil in Marseille, a mixture of joy and relief rushed through my veins. It felt terrific to be back on familiar turf.

We caught a train to Grenoble. It was a lovely city, offering a wealth of history among the old churches and a grandiose palace. The Alps surrounded the city providing stunning views in every direction. It was breathtaking. Still, Dawn chose not to stay, wanting to see Dijon. We moved on, at long last arriving in the place where I felt most at home.

Dawn decided she would like to stay in Dijon. I returned to living with the Devant's while she moved into a girls' dormitory on the university campus. We both signed up for the foreign students program. Dawn enrolled in one set of the program's classes while I chose a different group of classes. We began moving down separate paths.

A few weeks after my return, two letters arrived from my parents that would have a major influence on my experiences in France. The first contained many warm remarks from my mother along with a check. It was a modest sum by American standards, but in France, the money would pay my living expenses for the next three months. My parents had decided to support my studies and would send another check for the same amount around the Christmas holidays. Living a modest lifestyle, I could now manage to study without working.

The second letter was from my father. A short letter, he briefly informed me that the draft board wanted me to come in for a physical. He had notified them that I was living overseas and they were requesting more information regarding my whereabouts. The letter contained some forms for me to fill out. It was unclear whether or not being a student in a foreign country gave me student status in the United States. This was important as students were not being called into the armed services.

The French, having been driven out of Vietnam some years earlier, gave a lot of attention to the escalation taking place there. French newspapers consistently condemned the Americans as aggressors and imperialists. I believed the U.S. involvement in Southeast Asia was unjustified and wanted no part of a war. Still, I felt obliged to comply with the draft board's request as my dad recommended. I sent him the completed forms.

Since school did not begin for another month, I returned to my job at the lumber yard to earn some extra money, settling into a simple life. The student restaurant in town had already opened. Dawn and I got together for meals there only rarely. Boys were not allowed in the girls dormitories which put an end to our more intimate relations. Occasionally, Dawn and I spent Sundays hiking with the Devant family. I read and went on walks around Dijon in my spare time.

Living in Talant was pleasant, even easy. Unfortunately, it had become a little boring as well. Just before classes began, I moved back into the dormitories so I could pick out a room there ahead of the crowds. I liked the idea of being surrounded by students. Being a full time college student meant a lot to me. I felt proud of this new status.

There were a few more foreign students this year than last, but the mix of rich kids from big eastern American cities, South Americans and children of diplomats remained about the same. This time, I made more of an effort to avoid the American students from the outset. Dawn migrated towards them, quickly joining their ranks.

Most of the courses for foreign students were still held in the old classrooms downtown in those ancient stone buildings that I loved so much. The second year curriculum included classes in French art, history and literature. It also included a philosophy course. I zeroed in on that one, selecting philosophy as my core subject. I figured that way maybe I would become wise.

A few weeks into the school year, I had managed to establish casual friendships with a group of South Americans. Our group gathered in one corner of the campus café downstairs after evening meals for coffee and to practice our French.

One sunny fall afternoon as the lunch crowd left the building, I joined the Latin Americans in the downstairs café to listen and learn as they translated Spanish slang into French slang for fun. They kept thinking up more outrageous expressions, even improvised a few. The laughter grew until it echoed across the hall.

Suddenly from a nearby table, a burly character wearing a wrinkled sport coat and cotton shirt, its open collar askew, strolled over to our group. He was around six feet tall with unruly hair twisted across his head as if he hadn't slept or bothered to groom in days. His bushy eyebrows did little to restrain his big brown eyes that pressed forward as if trying to escape from their sockets. Those eyes sparkled with the same mischievous smile that filled his entire face.

"Hola caballeros, mucho gusto en conocerlos. Pero dígame hombres. ¿Donde están los bórdelos y las putanas? Quiero beber y mujer."

Everyone broke into laughter. I picked up on the words for brothel and whore. The rest escaped me. This strange person inserted himself with ease into the group. He continued

192

to talk, switching to speak in excellent French, his accent much better than my own. He spoke in a manner that was not quite native. As he talked on, I came to suspect that he was most likely German.

This fellow had the same gift as Félix to captivate a room full of people. Unlike Félix, he gave the impression of being slightly wild and unpredictable. He poked fun at the foreign student program for its stiff and conservative nature. He joked about all the forms and the limited choices offered in the curriculum while laughing and slapping people on the back. He made grand gestures careening about in the undersized plastic chair. Images of a grizzly scratching his back against a tree or plucking fish from the lake came to mind.

Although I kept quiet, he eventually got around to me. He said something in German to which I replied in French that I did not speak German. Without asking me where I was from, he changed back to French.

"Well, my friend, allow me to present myself, you are now in the company of Mr. Peter Lang," he smiled and stuck out his big hand. "Please accept this hand that I humbly offer in friendship."
Just as I reached for his hand, he added, "Remember my friend, if you shake this hand, it will be entirely at your own risk."
The others burst into laughter. As I shook his big hand, I scanned that face from ear to ear to better assess his intentions. What I found before me was an undeniable, if highly irreverent and impish, expression of delight.

New Beginnings
This year promised to be quite different than the previous one. Like manna from heaven, my parents' money liberat-

ed me from the struggle to pay basic bills. All my time and effort could now be focused on studies. This time, I had a real shot at passing the exams. There was even enough money to buy the books.

Digging into the task at hand, I purchased a Larousse French Dictionary written entirely in French Then I used my French /English dictionary to look up the French words that I didn't know in my Larousse Dictionary. These were French words used in the definitions of the French words that I had already looked up in all French dictionary. It became a most laborious way to arrive at an understanding. Yet, there were benefits. Grasping the meaning of a word through the connotations of other French words created a new depth of comprehension. Nuances in the cultural implications of words surfaced. Ideas broadened like light spreading into a spectrum as it passed through water. Reading French literature was becoming an extraordinary adventure.

Instead of that momentary flash of satisfaction from understanding the English translation of a word, larger images blossomed in my imagination. Words floated across my thoughts like sheer veils fluttering in the breeze through which glimpses of people, places, and passions could occasionally be captured. A new France was coming alive for me as described in the words of its greatest authors. This country that I found so nurturing, the people so compassionate, the system so safe and reassuring, was more complex than I had ever realized. I began to dream in French. Yet, no Frenchman like Félix came into my life that year. The only Frenchman who befriended me was a young man living in my dorm. He was a meek retiring sort named Martin. Thin and short, his narrow face struggled mightily to support a thick pair of glasses that extended beyond his hollow cheek bones. He often carried a book with him and liked to sit reading at the little desk in my room. Martin rarely spoke, content to just hang around. I recognized myself in him at some primordial level and felt most comfortable having him there.

Reading took me out of the world around me while bringing it closer in a different way. Books became templates that I could use to measure my surroundings. One of my favorites was Gustav Flaubert's *Madame Bovary*. Flaubert wrote about life in France one hundred years earlier. Yet, his descriptions of ordinary French people living provincial lives resembled the behavior and public interactions that took place all around me every day.

Flaubert captured many details of his characters' attitudes. He described their clothing, contrasting the kind of people they were with how they wanted the world to perceive them. Flaubert's insights into the way the French sized each other up based on appearances eclipsed time. He presented a society trapped in a series of oppressive codes of behavior that imposed narrowly defined roles. All that French politeness I had so admired also served to define the boundaries of assigned status that could not be crossed. What I had found so charming the year before, now took on an insular quality.

This new layer of France gradually evolved in my awareness. The sense of security born from deciphering how to behave in public came at a price. Even my place as *le grand American* began to seem like a cage. I had quickly learned how to fulfill this role and take some advantage from it. Yet, this was a parody that I not only felt expected to play, but could not easily escape. The inverse of Madame Bovary, who lived a prisoner in the confines of her status as the doctor's wife in a small town, I began to question my place in France. As a person outside the mainstream, I wondered just exactly what it meant to the French to be identified as this caricature of the visiting American. How did my performance measure up?

195

Reading about this other aspect of the society began to affect my outlook on life. I started to think of young people here as birds in cages, confined by the limited opportunities available in such an inbred homogeneous society. The decisions dictating how to conduct their lives were made by those close to them and bound by a rigid social order. They had little say.

Martin struck me as an embodiment of the French students' dilemma. He was not handsome. His ordinariness and lack of physical prowess would have marginalized him to some degree in an American school. The situation struck me as even less desirable in France, where young people lived subjected to the constant, often outspoken, judgments of their friends and family. There was little freedom for personal expression. Martin often looked downtrodden, burdened by this relegation to a role not of his choosing. He gave the outward impression of a dull sullen boy. Yet, his scholarly observations abounded with originality, ingenuity and wit.

Martin loved literature, art and poetry. He would help me with the definition of nuanced words and to understand how things worked in France. He described by what means the fate of a student was determined early in life. At the age of fourteen, the French school split in two groups directing some youth into apprenticeship classes for skilled labor while others prepared for college. Yet, Martin's explanations never got personal, never mentioned his village or family. Martin lived in his books; the important realm for Martin was that of the imagination. He preferred the company of foreigners like my new German friend Peter and me to the prescribed roles defined for him by society. We offered him escape, a brief moment of personal freedom. I understood perfectly.

Unlike Martin, Peter possessed vast resources of energy. It did not take long for the two of us to find common ground. Instantly likeable, I recognized in him the same adventuresome spirit that ran through all the German sailors I had known. Peter also knew a lot. A few years older than me, he had finished university and was taking a year to improve his knowledge of French culture. He had already read much of the classical French literature and spoke excellent French.

Peter didn't show up in any of my classes. Our paths crossed at the student café and around town. He could never be found before noon. Peter had solved his trouble sleeping at night by reading "Doc Savage" paperbacks until dawn before catching some rest. He dressed in respectable sports jackets and shirts, but never got them on quite straight. His appearance to others didn't bother him. I liked this detachment. It gave him a rebellious quality, that spark of independence.

When I did not understand a passage or concept in one of the books I was reading, I would seek Peter out. His unique interpretations of texts intrigued and helped me. He gradually became an important resource. Afternoons when I wasn't in the library, I could occasionally be found in Peter's room or him in mine discussing ideas. Martin was often there to help us both. New friendships were in the making.

Twiddle Dee and Twiddle Dum
One day as Peter and I loafed around the dorms with nothing much to do, I jumped into how the French almost always had a similar initial response to me as the American visitor.

"You know, Peter, the French usually react in a happy way when they first meet me. Oh, I have to tell them I don't like U.S. policies abroad. But after that, it's surprising how curious they are about America. They seem to want me to tell them about tall buildings and long streets. They can't

197

actually believe that all Americans eat only hamburgers and live in big houses, can they?"

"What did you expect? For most of these country kids, Dijon is the biggest city they have ever seen. Most have never been to Paris, much less America. What they know of America glows before them on the big screen. You represent glamour, Richard. You're freedom and hope. You're Hollywood."

"I don't mind much. They're nice to me."

"You're an escape, the exotic. You are the embodiment of hope."

"It's getting tiring, Peter. Sometimes I would just like to pass for another boring guy. I love it here. I want to suck this air into my lungs and fill myself with French life. But something's missing. I don't quite fit. If I did, it would probably be like Martin fits. He doesn't seem too happy." Peter replied, "That's the best part. You and I are free NOT TO BE FRENCH, to do as we please. We can choose to exercise our free will. *Vive l'acte gratuite!* The French see our shadows on the wall. It's up to us to make those shadows dance in any way we command."

Peter got me thinking. After all, most of the older generation of Frenchmen probably remembered my father's generation as benevolent liberators marching down the boulevards giving out candy. I could get away with things that Frenchmen never dared. I pictured myself non-threatening and instantly likeable. Maybe I did offer a temporary escape from the confines of the French social structures. It was a first impression that had helped me last year. Even if this superficial garb didn't really fit, it was not an especially heavy cloak to shoulder.

Germans, on the other hand, evoked a definite stereotype for Americans. I said to Peter, "You must cast a dark shadow on the walls of Dijon. When I grew up, all we knew about Germans came from pictures of men in tall boots, wearing stiff collars, carrying red flags with black swastikas. These were the scary ones, tough guys who stuck their arms straight out and marched across Europe. Even though we secretly admired their strength, we were taught to fear them. They were the bad guys."

Peter replied, "When I grew up in Berlin, we fashioned toys from chunks of shattered concrete. Not many dads could be seen in the neighborhood. Foreign soldiers divided up what remained of my city into controlled sectors. As a student, I watched the Russians cut us off and wall us in. Most of the boots parading down my street were on the feet of strangers. But don't focus on the walls my friend, rather on the light that flickers along the edges of the shadows giving them movement, bringing them to life."

This didn't make much sense. However, I understood Peter a little better. His love of live, his joy had prevailed in spite of the world around him. I remembered seeing the newsreels featuring aerial movies of the bombed out cities across Germany. They were triumphant news reports and none of them mentioned what happened after the bombs hit. In high school, I recalled more newsreels of the Berlin Wall and the airlift. While the French youth had grown up in the confines of a rigid society, Peter had grown up trapped in an international prison. We shared a desire to escape from the roles others would have us play. Peter and I found more common ground. We rejoiced at being free to enjoy ourselves, alive and well in France.
"What do the French think of you Peter, a German? The French must have some picture in their minds of what the typical German is like."

"Well Richard, we're European and it's a complicated situation. The war is long over and De Gaulle has extended his hand to Germany. The jester's suit I wear is woven from a mixture of strong threads, threads of respect, of intelligence, of order of efficiency, of fear and of hatred among other things. It's the way in which I shape these elements before the French that will determine how they follow the movements of my shadow."

"Hmmm, the German and the American jesters in Dijon, that could be an interesting combination," I thought out loud. Together, we could evoke all kinds of interesting reactions.

"The promise of individual freedom is only part of your shadow, *mon vieux*. Do you know what else the French call you Americans? *Les grands enfants* meaning undisciplined, uneducated, and unable to control your emotions, in a word, uncivilized, that's also a part of your jester suit. Another vestment of your outfit casts a deeper shadow, that of *l'enfant sauvage*. Yes, Americans also evoke the image of the wild child fresh from the forest raised by beasts."

"How will you make your shadow dance my friend? Be prepared to expect the unexpected from actions taken in the Land of Serendipity. Never forget, even if they cage you in with high walls, the spirit is free, *liberté, egalité, fraternité*," Peter gave me one of his devilish smiles. Some of this made sense. It wasn't unusual for Peter to string together words that seemed more like distant cousins than brothers. Yet, his ideas triggered my own inventiveness. A German and an American working in tandem could open a few doors. I imagined us exploring the sleepy provincial town of Dijon seeking out uncertain adventure like Don Quixote and Sancho Panza fearlessly conquering windmills.

A Great Feast

It didn't take long for Peter to tire of living in the dorms. Rather than look for housing through the Student Services Office, he posted an advertisement in the local newspaper. I had no idea that was possible. Whatever Peter wrote in that ad, it worked wonders for he was contacted by the Councilor of Finland who offered to rent Peter a room next to his personal residence in the same building that lodged the Consulate offices.

It was a terrific location near the center of town in a neighborhood lined with elegant buildings. Peter's room had a window that opened to the street. His private entrance tucked into one side of the stone archway that led to a small courtyard. It was a nice big room with a sink and large bed; it had an air of luxury. The only significant drawback lay in its visibility from the concierge's lodgings directly across the courtyard.

The French concierge represented a formidable force in those days. These women, by tradition matronly women, would put any modern day security system to shame. They were always out cleaning the courtyard or sitting by their large windows. The concierge station was typically strategically located to allow for full range surveillance of the courtyard and entryway. These ladies greeted everyone amicably keeping up on the latest events in their tenants' lives.

They were often quite helpful. At the same time, little escaped their watchful eye. They seemed to know the whereabouts of all residents most of the time, as well as, many intimate details of their lives. The landlord had only to chat with them to keep up on both the needs of the building and activities of his lodgers. Any concierge could provide the landlord with excellent detailed Intel in the event some wrongdoing needed to be addressed. She served as an important guardian of public morals.

Shortly after Peter moved in, the Councilor General acknowledged his arrival with a dinner invitation. It would seem that as an extension of his duties in Dijon, the Councilor frequently held large dinner parties. With some friendly cajoling, Peter was able to secure me an invitation as well. This sociable Finish official most likely thought a curious pair of students from America and Germany would make for interesting dinner guests.

Nothing could have prepared me for the feast that followed. The early hour at which the evening was to begin did seem out of keeping with tradition. We were asked to arrive at six o'clock on a Saturday afternoon. In France at that time, the evening meal normally began closer to eight o'clock. I had the good sense to wear my only coat and tie for the occasion.

The Councilor's private rooms were on the second floor overlooking the courtyard. We gathered in a parlor adorned with century old furniture and Persian rugs. Dark oil paintings hung on the walls. A large bar had been set up in one corner next to a row of ceiling-high windows and glass paned doors. An iron railed terrace silhouetted the courtyard below.

Formal greetings proliferated as some ten or twelve people entered the room. Most looked much older than me and were far more stylishly dressed. Peter jumped right in, displaying his usual swagger and testing the waters with talk of the new economic ties to Germany and De Gaulle's mighty Fifth Republic. This led Peter into his furrowed brow, dropped jaw and guttural imitation of the Great General's unmistakable voice. Peter mimicked De Gaulle as well as any French student. This always drew laughter. While Peter charmed our hosts, I settled back with a small glass of vermouth focusing on the only other young people in the room. A reasonably attractive mademoiselle around my age stood across the parlor talking to a young man. In a room full of adults, the thought of just going over and butting into a conversation between her and her friend without an introduction was intimidating, especially in such a formal atmosphere. I stayed put.

A lady wearing a dark apron emerged from the kitchen to whisper in the Councilor's ear. In a loud voice, he invited us all to enter the dining room. Leaving the parlor, I gazed at the space before me. Suddenly, I sensed that a journey across the centuries lay only a few steps ahead.
This dining hall had no windows. It extended some twenty-five feet in length. The space was narrow, about ten feet wide, with lofty ceilings. Looking up, I discovered a pageant of cherubs circling in a blue sky framed by white molding. Tapestries from the sixteenth and seventeenth centuries completely covered all four walls. Only the main entrance and kitchen door remained without covering.

These dense hangings depicted pastoral scenes, ladies with baskets of fruit, knights on horseback carrying lances, hawks, long robed women with angel's wings, even unicorns. The fading tapestries' surfaces only added to this ethereal reminder of a regal Europe. Above the mahogany table which seated at least fifteen, two crystal chandeliers hanging from white plaster medallions filled the room with an airy radiance. I felt myself entering into a dream state. The table settings hinted at a culinary adventure on a grand scale. A white porcelain plate lay centered between three forks on the left and an assortment of knives and spoons on the right. A row of small spoons rested above the plate. Four wine glasses arranged slightly to the right above the plates added to the promise of delight. A white linen napkin at the center of this array held in a roll by a thick silver ring counseled patience until the word was given to begin. I felt my self confidence shrinking as my brain compressed into a tiny knot, my clothes seemed shabby. I started to slouch. My only hope lay in complete silence. Maybe I had come through the wrong door and should be eating in the kitchen with the dishwashers. I scrutinized the other guests as they entered the room. The men wore well pressed suits, starched white shirts and stylish ties. Expensive looking jewelry encircled the necks of the ladies. With any luck, no one would talk to me. If I were really fortunate the others would not notice me at all.

Once the guests had settled into their seats around the table, our host offered a few words, "It's a pleasure to welcome you all here tonight. We have with us representatives of two continents and several important trading partners. An excellent meal awaits us thanks to the fine *cuisine* my chef, Antoine D'Aubigne. We have the good fortune to reside in the *centre gastronomic* of all of France. So without further delay, I invite you all to leave business affairs for another day. Tonight's a time to eat, drink and be merry."

Two waiters in uniforms wearing white gloves brought in the appetizers. A tray of *Gratinée de Coquille St Jacques* neatly sculptured onto large white seashells, steam swirling up from its golden brown crusts. It seemed to me that doors to paradise were beginning to open. Two other waiters circled the hall filling the first of our wine glasses with Chablis from bottles wrapped in white linen.

As the white shells revealed their scalloped centers and voices grew louder, the waiters standing at each corner of the room began removing dishes. Two of the waiters soon returned carrying fresh plates of sautéed perch in a delicate parsley lemon sauce. While the second pair of waiters followed circling the tables filled everyone's glass with a lightly chilled *Pouilly Fuissé*. The perch went down easily, helped by this smooth white wine.
After a few glasses of wine, I began to feel a little more relaxed. I started to enjoy this sumptuous adventure and wondered where it would end. As the waiters removed the remaining bones of perch, I sipped wine and contemplated

the considerable array of glasses and utensils still spread before me.

How different this was from the roast beef, mashed potatoes and gravy my mother served up. No sound of coffee percolating could be heard. Green peas wandering into the brown gravy would be out of place on this shiny porcelain. What wine would go well with green peas I wondered? At least, I knew to hold the fork with my left hand and work the knife with my right in the French manner. All was not lost, but it was going to be a long night.

Out came the waiters again bringing plates of veal cutlets looking magazine perfect. The veal surrounded by zucchini slices arranged on a bed of quartered mushrooms gently descended before me. The second team of waiters collected the white wine glasses. They returned to fill our next set of wide rimmed glasses from bottles of Bordeaux. Once again, the even taste of the gentle red wine blended perfectly into the light flavor of tender veal. My mind was starting to float. I settled back listening to the conversation, still afraid to speak.

The man next to me was engaging his lady companion in a discussion of a film recently shown in town called, "Last Year at Mariennbad." It had come out a few years before and was playing at the artsy revival cinema in town. He raved about the brilliant blending of truth and illusion to create a dream world. According to my neighbor, this film cleverly manipulated time and events in such a way as to represent an evolution in the art of cinema. I had seen that film. It told no story, it made no sense. The images kept breaking up, variations of the same dull scene of people standing in a sterile courtyard trying to look mysterious played over and over. This picture bored me so much that it became painful to stay to the end. I considered jumping into the conversation, but doubted they wanted to hear my opinion.

Just when I thought the main course had ended and the final plates were being removed, out came more meat. Waiters appeared carrying my favorite French dish *boeuf bourguignon*. The second team soon returned with fresh bottles of *Pommard*, my favorite of the deep Burgundy reds. It seemed too good to be true.

I had sampled this and many other fine Burgundies during a visit to *Les Hospices de Beaune* last year, but could never afford such luxurious wines. This full bodied red wine brought out the richness of this thick sauce for beef. The combination was exquisite. I began to suspect this was all a dream.

Peter came into focus across the table holding his glass extended before him. In a high spirited voice he announced. "I propose a toast to our generous host, to excellent food and to these fine wines that stimulate conversation." He raised his glass inviting all to join him. He took a drink of wine and declared, 'When I drink, I think and when I think, I drink.' Appreciative laughter bounced around the dining room.

Someone across the table responded, "Remember, always run after a dog, he'll never bite you; always drink before thirst, and it will never overtake you". More laughter broke out. People were decidedly loosening up.

By the time we had cut deep into the cheese board, eaten our way through a fresh salad, cleansed our palates with sherbet and washed down the fruits with champagne, we contentedly arrived at the strawberry tarts and cream pastries. All that remained of my array of goblets was a lonely champagne glass. My head was beginning to wobble, pulling against my well anchored belly full of food. I no longer made any attempt to understand the chorus of lively chatter that filled the room. Voices echoed in my ears like hypnotic incantations.

The clock struck nine in the evening just before the Councilor decided to examine the American. Even though he sat some distance away at the head of the table, his regard clearly focused on me, "Well, Monsieur Richard, tell us about your great country. Are there still cowboys roaming the ranges and vast open lands? Does everyone drive big cars and own appliances of convenience as we hear tell? What is it like west of Washington?"

I started to feel deficient and a little defensive at being cast once again as the visiting American. How nice it would have been to remain quietly in the background. I was on the spot. The Councilor was clearly an experienced man. I remembered what Peter had told me about how the European's caricatured Americans. Was the Councilor playing with me? The rebel in me itched to get out, but I felt obliged to answer my host calmly. Besides, I lacked the refined wit needed to offer a clever reply.
"I guess it's true, the stuff about the big cars and appliances. When it comes to wilderness, well, we've got grizzlies running around the parks of the Blue Ridge Mountains. That's definitely true. Back home, when I was a boy, my dad chased a brown bear into those Tennessee hills one time."

I couldn't bring myself to leave well enough alone and continued right into troubled waters, "I guess it's true we're mostly simple, unsophisticated folk. I grew up drinking soda right out of the can and never knew it was rude to go barefoot in town or eat a hotdog while walkin' down the road. I even saw postcards from Texas of jack rabbits as big as horses. We're a kind of free spirited crowd where I come from. Maybe a little wild, I guess." I managed to stop myself from saying anything more.

Some around the table found my comments mildly amusing. After a short silence, the other guests went back to their various conversations. Failing to impress anyone did not disappoint me. I had fulfilled my duty and was relieved that the focus shifted elsewhere. Cutting off a piece of glazed strawberry tart then spearing it on my fork, I washed it down with a sip of champagne. To my surprise, their flavors complimented one another quite nicely.

The waiters began to tidy up when the Councilor invited us to move back into the parlor for cognac and cigars. Smoking had always made me dizzy, but on this occasion free cigars sounded just dandy. Since everything else went together so well, why not cognac and cigars? I attempted to settle into a straight backed chair with elaborately carved arms and a complicated needlework cushion.

Leaning back against a figure playing a lute to serenade his damsel, I watched the waiter pour a shot of cognac and set it on the Venetian inlaid humidor next to me. The Councilor circulated around the room offering all the men cigars. He came to me last. As I took one, he said, "All this European history must seem striking to you. Your country is so young. Do you know how the French describe you Americans? They call you *les grands enfants.*"

"Ah yes, *les grands enfants* that's us alright." I could feel myself losing it. "We just don't seem to care what anyone thinks about us as we go along our merry way. Actually, some folks consider us to be vulgar. But, you know what? We just enjoy life. We like to get comfortable and don't worry too much what the world thinks." Just as the Councilor settled into his big chair, I grabbed my cognac snifter in one hand, my cigar in the other and slid the humidor in front of me with my right foot. I put both feet up on the antique humidor, slouched down in the chair and said, "We Americans like to get REAL comfortable while we enjoy a good drink and a smoke. Now this is more like it." I smiled my rebel smile at the Councilor. This would most likely be my last invitation to one of his dinners.

A nervous laugh rippled across the room and quickly vanished. After only a few minutes, I started to feel really dumb and took my feet down returning the humidor to its place. Retreating back into a low profile, I enjoyed the last of the cognac waiting anxiously for the evening to end. After what seemed like an eternity, the party finally began to break up. Just before Peter and I headed out the door, the young lady I had been eyeing all evening and her friend came over to us. The girl spoke in a low voice.

"Would you two like to come to a party? It will begin next Friday evening around eight o'clock in the apartments just across the street on the second floor. This party won't be so stuffy. You're both invited." She turned to me and whispered in my ear in English, "We know a way to make you feel real comfortable!"

Dancing with Desire
Since most of my youth in America had been spent in the company of males, it was a world I understood. I was surrounded by male cousins, uncles and friends. We almost never played with girls. With the move to California, females became even more remote, unapproachable aliens. I began to suspect that they spoke another dialect of English where words held obscure meanings. Speaking words in their direction only resulted in distorted messages like light is bent and dispersed as it passes through water. It was not possible to communicate anything beyond the most simplest of needs. Theirs was a universe with strange incomprehensible rules and inaccessible mysteries.

My experiences in Australia had done little to advance my understanding the opposite sex. Things began to improve after meeting Dawn in Israel. I learned that women could be great companions. I feared them less. Inspired by Peter's boundless courage when approaching girls, I forged ahead into new intrigues. During this second year in Dijon,

209

I began to appreciate that not only did these fascinating creatures come in many shapes and sizes, but each young lady I met possessed wonderful and unique charms as different from one another as any two young men. It all started shortly after the Councilor of Finland's marvelous dinner.

Three's a crowd:
Her name escapes me. Surely, she had a name, but it doesn't really matter since who she really was will forever elude me. She undoubtedly introduced herself to me at the Councilor of Finland's dinner and again the following Friday evening when Peter and I arrived at her party. What I do know is that she had a secret.

Her party got off to a dull start. Peter and I arrived an hour late to find a group of a dozen or so young people standing around looking awkward. It would have been difficult to talk over the noisy French rock and roll music playing on the record player. We grabbed some punch, found a couple of chairs and began to wonder why our host claimed this would be such a great party. Just as we were getting tired of sitting around, the girl from the Councilor's dinner came over.

She spoke to us softly in French, "This isn't the real party; my girlfriend just arrived and if you'll come with us, we'll take you to the good party."

We followed them downstairs, hopped into her small *deux cheveaux*, a flimsy tin can of a car. We headed towards the country. Peter sank into the front bucket seat, while I slid close to our hostess in the back. After a half hour bouncing over country roads in the dark, we arrived at a gated country manor. It was a two story stone building, just shy of qualifying as a modest castle. A strange mix of shiny BMWs and Citroën luxury sedans were parked next to road-weary economy cars around the circular driveway.

210

As we walked through the door we encountered a salacious cast of characters reminiscent of the Sydney waterfront. A dozen or so people wondered around sipping wine. The women were in various stages of undress. Some women that I could just make out on the second balcony seemed to be naked. The men upstairs had their shirts off or wore only underwear. One woman clad in white panties and a fancy white bra sashayed towards me. Her eyes sizing me up with a hungry stare.

People danced on a large floor off to my left. My new girl headed in that direction to dance with a man twice her age. As I watched, he held her very close while sliding his hand across her bottom. Just as the lady in the white bra reached out to secure the object of her desire, I saw red. Strutting over like Mister Macho, I pushed the dirty old man away from my girl. "This is my girl came with me to the party. Find your own girl!" I stared him down trying to seem tough.

Immediately, "my girl" grabbed me by the arm. Peter and I were both quickly shuffled back into the car. Before I knew what happened, the girl and I were in the back seat again heading toward Dijon. I wasn't giving up. If it was an orgy the girls wanted, why not here and now. I began to try to kiss my partner and slid my hand up her dress.

To my surprise, she turned her head away arching back against the seat. Not only were my kisses rejected, but as I slid my hand further up her dress, I ran into an impenetrable object. It felt like some kind of heavy garment made of thick rubber and bulky fibrous cloth. I tried to reach above it, but the thing encased her whole stomach. This synthetic chastity belt provided bulletproof protection. I collapsed in confused defeat. Why did she wear this kind of armor to an orgy and what was I thinking? My girl! I didn't even know this girl!

Peter and I wound up unceremoniously dumped on the sidewalk at the edge of town as the girls sped off at a breakneck pace back to the country manor. How could I have been so dumb? Why did I care who this crazy girl danced with? Where did this knee jerk morality come from? Why couldn't I stop myself from behaving like a country bumpkin? I slunk back to the dorms in a cutting wind as the snow melted against my face. I felt alone and dejected. I told myself that what happened didn't matter since I could never be comfortable with a band of nude strangers. The only good thing was that Peter didn't get mad at me for messing up his chances. Peter was good that way; he knew how to handle defeat.

The Indomitable Phantom:
Brigitte, now there is a name I will never forget. If I close my eyes, I can still see the sliver crucifix hanging seductively against her smooth skin. She was wearing a black cotton dress with a v-cut neckline. Even after I removed her dress, that silver cross glistened between her breasts, shining brilliantly in contrast to her straight black hair and dark brown eyes.

We met in the student cafeteria one day. She had grown up in Dijon and lived there with her parents. She also had the grace to not jump right in with a bunch of dumb questions about America. I appreciated that. We met over coffee a few times, went for a few walks. Even though ours did not qualify as a great romance, we got along well, felt comfortable together. A physical attraction definitely existed between us as did the sexual tension which came in ever stronger waves.

Her parents presented a significant obstacle due to their strict oversight. They would not let her stay out after dark. One day, Peter arranged for me use his room in the after-

212

noon. Brigitte seemed excited at the idea of an illicit rendezvous. The day finally arrived. Peter managed to distract the concierge, while Brigitte and I slipped through the side door. We only had a few hours. I closed the heavy wooden shutters and slid the curtains across them.

The top layer of clothes came off quickly. We did a lot of passionate kissing. This time I was not going to allow my mother to be present. Emboldened by the desire I could read in Brigitte's eyes, my hands ventured out in brazen defiance of Protestant morality. I explored many wonderful curves and crevices. The room became steamy and filled with delicious odors.

In spite of all this rapture, something went wrong. Brigitte resisted any attempt to remove her undergarments. She clearly enjoyed our passionate embraces while at the same time she seemed to struggle with her own conscience. Her face twisted into expressions of suffering. Like Briar Rabbit punching the Tar Baby, every new erotic touch bound us together rendering escape as difficult as consummation. After an eternity, we managed to struggle apart, dressed and slipped quietly from the room. This experience brought up all the unanswered questions about what happened between Vera and me in Israel. Brigitte and I built an invisible wall between us that day.
We continued to see one another, but less and less frequently. I would occasionally walk her home. Unfortunately, she lived down the road form Peter. Every time we passed by that apartment, her face contorted into the same disturbed grimace revealing both pain and pleasure. We never talked about what had happened nor could we put the experience behind us.

Constant Love:
Joelle was cut from another cloth; hers was not a suffering God. A plaque just over her bed read, *Oui, c'est etre constant que d'aimer l'amour*. In English, "It is to be constant,

213

to love love. I never quite understood what that meant. The word *constant* lay at the root of the problem.

This word implied a lot of ideas in French, not just the concept of being consistent. It meant being reliable, dependable even held the high ground of being a person with impeccable moral convictions. There was also an earthly connotation hinting at a physical hardness. The expression, *d'aimer l'amour*, to love love, also suggested more than one interpretation. A person could love being romantically, even spiritually, in love, but they could also just love making love.

Joelle approached life in an equally complicated and somewhat duplicitous way. She only allowed me to see her during the week as her steady boyfriend came to town on the weekends. Joelle preferred that I arrive well after sunset and leave before sunrise. She often woke me up several times during the night to make love, only to complain in the morning that I slept all the time. The odd thing is that I can't remember much of anything about our love making. What I do remember is the exceptional strength Joelle exhibited for such a willow of a girl. She clung to me through the night flexing every muscle, her arms and legs wrapped so tightly around me that I couldn't move.

One morning, I got out of bed to dress only to discover that my underwear had gone missing. "Joelle, where are my shorts?" I demanded.

"I hid them. You deserve to loose them for being such a lazy boy. The cold morning air will make your butt shiver, wake you up. You'll walk faster and work harder," she smiled her nymph's smile.

When I came close to finding my briefs, she grabbed them and started running around the room squealing. I ran around the room naked chasing the rascal until I finally caught her. I put my shorts on, while we both laughed. Too soon, that fatal day finally arrived when her steady boy-

friend moved back to town. While it lasted, Joelle made
lovemaking seem like child's play.
Nectar of the Gods:

Marie Claire was the studious type. I first saw her in the
ancient municipal library. This magnificent edifice offered
sanctuary in the heart of Dijon's historic center where narrow streets snaked between centuries old stone buildings.
A heavy oak door as wide as the street opened into the library's dimly lit central room.

Passing over the threshold, I entered the imposing cham-
ber, where a vaulted ceiling loomed high overhead. Two
stories of stone arches stretched out on either side of the
central floor. Set back from the main hall under the arches,
deep alcoves housed most of the books. Stacks of leather
bound books with imposing black and brown seams were
neatly arranged on the oak bookcases which stood high
against the walls.

The second story offered the eerie spectacle of two long
rows of balconies that towered over the main floor. Their
cascading rows of shallower arches framed murky caverns.
On the main floor, long maple study tables arranged in
rows were divided by two narrow aisles. The tables were
divided into several workstations lit by brass lamps with
large brown shades evenly spaced along the table's surface. Each lamp cast a small circle of golden rays. Each
workstation offered its own little umbrella of light that
shed a thin glow only a few feet before yielding to the
shadowy surroundings.

I loved to study in this serene place. One day, I spotted
Marie Claire quietly reading. The way the pale light re-
flected off her blond hair made it hard to distinguish be-
tween strands hair and rays of light. She had a classic
Greek beauty with high cheek bones and fine features.
Shadows played against the light accentuating the planes

215

of her face adding a glamorous air. She was the most beautiful girl I had ever seen. She could have been sitting in that chair one hundred years earlier in this same library from a bygone era and her beauty would still have been considered exquisite. In that moment, in that place, her perfection overwhelmed me. Marie Claire lifted me out of myself.

It took many afternoons of returning to study in the old library before Marie Claire noticed me. Finally, I got up the nerve to talk to her. She was mildly friendly at first. As our encounters continued, she became more relaxed and talked about her home town in the wine country. One day she let me walk her back to her dorm.

Marie Claire lived in the old dorms downtown in the ivy covered stone buildings next to the old cafeteria. These dorms were strictly monitored. Even though boys were not allowed, she let me walk her up to her floor. In the hallway, I kissed her briefly and hugged her. As I felt her wonderful body press against mine, I pulled her close and kissed the nape of her neck. An extraordinarily sensual perfume filled my nostrils sending a shiver of excitement down my whole body. I relaxed pulling back enough to see her face and asked, "What is that perfume you are wearing? It is wonderful!"

She gave me a surprised stare, "I'm not wearing any perfume." Then she looked around nervously. "You better leave now before you get me in trouble."

I walked Marie Claire back to her dorms a few more times after that but never again made it up to the second floor. She was too perfectly beautiful, always a little aloof. It was impossible for me to get beyond my own feelings of unworthiness around her. In the days to come, we saw very little of each other; she never even came close to being a girlfriend.

216

Yet, thanks to Marie Claire. I discovered a whole new vision of womanhood. Just being around her lifted my spirits to a new place of reverence. When I walked at her side, it became an out-of-body experience. The joy I felt in her company left me speechless and awkward. She rose to a status that no other girl had ever reached. Perhaps it was because I never got to know her well. Perhaps the limited physical contact had something to do with it. Whatever the reason, Marie Claire, and her perfume, ascended to mythical heights in my universe. She transformed my previously earthly image of woman into that of an ideal creature who walked with the gods. She became impossible to ever forget.

The Illusive Nature of Wisdom
School provided infinitely more satisfaction this year than last. With my days freed to read and discover, I tackled the task of learning full of enthusiasm. My literature and art classes moved along nicely as more of the subtle qualities of French society continued to come into focus. The French language grew wings carrying me to new places of beauty. I discovered the seemingly simple poetry of Jacque Prévert. When I heard it put to song by Yves Montand, I was transported by its power to create beautiful images that took on a life of their own.
My core subject of philosophy, however, proved to be considerably more daunting than expected. I was looking forward to gaining some wisdom so I could become more like those San Francisco Beatniks. To my surprise, the road to acquiring wisdom wound through vast volumes of tedious text. It did not flow or create wonderful images of people and places. This writing contained no interesting descriptions of life at all.

Things started well enough. Descartes was the first great thinker whose works I took on. My first impressions came

217

from a particular painting of him. Maybe it was the only image of him, because the same portrait kept popping up in every text. The face that glared out at me exposed a man who looked as if he would take pleasure in spitting on my head while I kissed his feet. He struck me as a bureaucrat's bureaucrat. A finer picture of arrogance would have been hard to find.

Still, I understood this guy. I could even understand why he needed to behave in such a haughty manner. I learned that he lived in a time when the Vatican ruled with the heavy hand of the Inquisition. People offering explanations of the universe that conflicted with the Catechism had their jaws crushed in a vise or were burned at the stake in the town square. It took enormous arrogance to mess with Pope Urban VIII.

Descartes dared to propose a new way of analyzing phe- nomenon using experimentation to verify facts. This way of thinking came naturally to me. After all, my father was a scientist for whom everything was logical. He taught us that the laws of nature explained the universe. My brother and I learned with chemistry sets that gave us the ability to change clear fluids into many colors simply by mixing them. We could stink up an entire room with sulfur or make powders explode. We became experts in reading lit- mus paper. In my home, Dad taught us the laws of physics the way priests dictated instructions from the Catechism. Descartes was the father of analytical geometry. My dad would have liked him.

I began to have my first doubts about gaining wisdom when I attempted to read Descartes' long treatises. I dis- covered that I had difficulty with the way he used lan- guage. Descartes' famous statement *je pense donc je suis* (I think therefore I am) formed the starting point for his ex- planation of the world. It sounded so simple, so easy to read. I thought I understood it.

Yet, the more I read the thick volumes elaborating on the meaning of those words, the more the connection between thinking and being became obscure. I struggled through laborious texts explaining in great detail what had at first appeared to be a simple phrase. The more I read, the more I became snarled in the logic. Mostly, my eyes got sore and my head hurt. I sat confused, reading the same sentence over and over.

I took to studying other scholars' explanations of Descartes until I felt pretty comfortable with the general ideas of his philosophy. But those few words, "I think, therefore I am," continued to bother me. I did not trust that I really understood what they meant.

Descartes must have belonged to the same club as the other philosophers in the course. They all seemed to have these catch phrases that were supposed to somehow illuminate the secrets of the world. I never felt comfortable with any of these guys. Wisdom seemed to lay scattered across thousands of big words that must be put together like a giant jigsaw puzzle and none of the pieces lined up very well in my head. Philosophy took on the appearance of an exclusive endeavor that thrived only in the lofty heights of scholarly study and had little to do with ordinary people like me.

As winter loosened its grip on the land, we came to Jean-Paul Sartre and the existentialists. This was the guy that the Beatniks worshiped. My attention heightened; my enthusiasm was renewed. Sartre differed from his predecessors. He wrote popular novels to develop his philosophy. I felt hopeful that at last I could learn his lessons of wisdom in a more direct way. Right after that first class on existentialism, I walked over to the bookstore and bought a copy of *La Nausee (Nausea)*, one of his earliest and most famous novels.

My first feeling of foreboding came when I turned the paperback over. A picture of Sartre filled the back cover. He sat at a desk, his face filling most of the picture. This man looked very sad. His features were round and full; his head almost too big for his body. His big eyes stared out above puffy pillows of flesh and just below a pair of bushy eyebrows. Those eyes were magnified by bulky glasses that rode down on his wide nose. A black pipe dangled from a pair of unusually thick lips. Sartre reminded me of a bullfrog, still and melancholic, looking out over a bleak pond full of dead fish.

"Nausea" turned out to be the story of a pathetic character named Antoine. Early on in the story, an odd thing happened; he became afraid of a stone. Stones had never frightened me. In the first chapter, he went to a café and the local prostitute had sex with him for free when she was not busy. That's when I first began to suspect Sartre was not so wise. Any sailor knew that prostitutes never put out for free.

Everything around him made Antoine sick; women disappointed him. Antoine spiraled down hill fast. Even a little fog frightened him. I loved to walk in the fog. One day, he hopped a tram where some creep stretched out on the bench across from him scared the daylights out of Antoine. He rushed off the tram, plopped down on a park bench in an attempt to escape nausea only to discover the chestnut tree next the bench made him want to vomit. Suddenly, a veil was torn away and Antoine got wisdom. Sartre never explained with much clarity what made up the nature of that wisdom.

I tried my best to catch his wisdom. Sartre continued in the next few pages about half-way houses, non-existence, flaunting abundance and being in the way for eternity. Subjects that didn't go together all that well in my head. He went on for several more pages of twists and jumps be-

220

fore Antoine wound up deciding that contingency is essential. *Contingency is essential*, what did this mean?

The following few pages were even more bewildering. I began to doubt philosophy delivered much wisdom. Trying not to become too discouraged by the book, I decided Sartre had to be wise. After all he was so famous and the Beatniks worshiped him.

One grey morning, I bundled up and went out to the park. I walked until I found a skeletal tree whose big branches looked imposing. I settled onto the bench across from the tree. Staring at the tree for a long time, I tried to make myself feel like vomiting. I tried to pull wisdom from the tree, to become contingent.

Other than starting to get cold, I couldn't feel the least bit sick. I definitely did not feel like vomiting. The tree did not scare me, no matter how hard I tried to picture it as frightening. After a half hour or so, a few rays of sunlight broke through the overcast sky. As they warmed me up, I began to get hungry. Remembering that the student cafeteria had just opened, I wandered down the path leading from the park toward the dorms.

As I walked, I wondered what Sartre meant by his key phrase; *existence precedes essence*. The more I thought about it, the less sense it made. I begin to wonder what the Beatniks liked so much about this guy. I started to suspect that they might be a bunch of phonies. Maybe Beatniks weren't special.

Sam Needs You

As the snow flurries turned to rain, I received word from my father that he had, once again, been contacted by the draft board. They were requesting that I report for a physical in some army base outside of Paris.

221

The whole business of conscription and the war was never far from my thoughts. Some nights I tossed in my bed struggling with what to do if they called me up for duty. I pretty much believed French papers that condemned the U.S. actions in Vietnam. My best experiences had been in foreign countries and there was no way I was going to volunteer to kill Vietnamese people in this distant land. The domino theory that my government offered as a justification seemed ridiculous. Yet, my father expected me to behave respectably. I would keep my appointment at the base, Camps De Loges.

Catching a train headed north, I set out for a place called Rocquencourt near Versailles where the US Army base was located. After a few metro changes and a long bus ride, I stepped onto the edge of a field across from the base. It was an uninviting location with low rolling plains. A crisp wind bounced across the grey earth. The guards in the gate house greeted me warmly as they had in Madrid. However, their attitude changed when they saw my induction paper. Acting as if they were already my superiors, they barked at me to wait outside. My angry muscles pulled taut.

These young men, close to my own age, appeared impatient to taunt the potential new recruit before them. They hustled me through the gates and ordered me to report to a building across the yard. Crossing a wide section of concrete pavement, I arrived at a drab box of a building. I entered into an office stacked with black steel file cabinets and grey metal desks that looked like leftovers from World War II. The clerk studied my letter. He handed me a clipboard full of forms mumbling at me to complete them. I sat down on one of the metal chairs resting on the marbled-grey linoleum floor. Leaning against a pale green wall, I began to complete the forms.

The second form I uncovered was a questionnaire requiring me to list the address of every place I had lived since the age of sixteen. I scribbled away, writing above and below the straight lines in train wreck cursive. A growing bitterness simmered in me at being in this dreary place and bossed around by a bunch of dim-witted auto-bots. There would have been a time, not so long ago, when these people would have intimidated me. I would have thought them my betters. Not any longer. They probably couldn't even speak French like the Vietnamese. Shortly after I finished angrily scratching out my signature on the last page, the office door swung open and a voice from within called out authoritatively. "Come in here young fellow."

A strong looking older man wearing a uniform with a few extra badges pinned to his chest and stripes on his shoulders demanded my clipboard. I noticed a plaque on his desk that read *Sergeant Riley*.
"Sit down, kid, while I look this over."

I dropped onto another of those hard metal chairs and waited. He pressed slowly back against his chair as he flipped to that second questionnaire on the clipboard. His chair had cushioned arm rests. It sat taller than mine. He paused to carefully peruse through the pages of this particular form with a suspicious look in his eye.
"What are you doing in France?" he questioned curiously, sounding as if he thought I wasn't supposed to be here.
"I'm a student at the l'Univeristé de Dijon." I replied using my best French accent to name the school. How was his French accent? I wondered if he even spoke French.

His eyes moved down the page, "What were you doing in Australia?" His face curled into a stern expression.
"Working"
"Well, how did you get to Australia?"
"A German freighter"

"A German freighter, what the hell were you doing on a German freighter?"

"Working"

He paused for a moment, "And how did you get to France?"

"German freighter"

"Working on that one too, I suppose." He looked at me with distrust. "What the hell did you do for a whole year in Australia?"

"Mostly, I worked at Callan Park"

"And what exactly is Callan Park?"

"An insane asylum"

This skeptical character fixed me in his gaze for a long moment. His expression of disbelief was reinforced by an angry stare. Evidently, he decided not to explore the details of my job at the asylum as he turned back to study my paperwork.

While he looked away, I decided to give him the French once over. His uniform stood stiff and spotless, the collar rode high against his thick neck. His brass buttons shone like new coins. Not a wrinkle could be found along the line where his shirt disappeared into the waist line. The only odd part, which struck me as almost comical, was his haircut. He looked like one of those Ohio farm boys whose mother took a shears to his head and razor cut the rest with a salad bowl on his noggin.

"And what about these addresses? There are months unaccounted for in here. Take Israel, this past summer, for example. What the hell were you doing in Israel and where did you stay there for three months? Are you Jewish?"

"No."

"Then, why did you stay in Israel for so long and why didn't you put an address on this form?" He was getting exited again.

224

"I just wanted to see the place. I moved around a lot, stayed in a tent on the beach for a month or so. It didn't really have an address."

"Worked in an insane asylum there, too, did you?" his voice filled with sarcasm.

"No, I worked for the Pakistanis' in Solomon's mines." He didn't bother to ask me about Solomon's mines. Silence filled the little office as he quit asking questions and finished searching through the remainder of my paperwork.

"We're going to have to see about this. I'll consult with some of the folks here about you. Be back in my office tomorrow morning at nine a.m. sharp."

"Okay, but I came all the way here form Dijon and have no place to stay. Do you mind if I spend the night somewhere on base? It would be easier to be on time tomorrow."

"Not unless you want to enlist right now. I have a tent you can sleep in then." He stared me down with a defiant smile.

I looked away, "No thanks, I'll be back in the morning." Leaving his office, I turned in my base pass at the gate and headed across the road. It had been a pain getting here on the bus. I didn't feel much like trekking all the way back to Paris just to return in the morning. The sky was overcast, but not the kind of clouds that promised rain. Looking around the area, I found a tree in a secluded part of the field and settled in for the night. The evening was a bit chilly, but I had a warm coat, wool socks and my gloves. It was not going to be easy to sleep with all the trucks rumbling down the highway.

The prospect of joining the army filled my thoughts. It would certainly be no fun to work for these guys, so arrogant and pushy. All those rules and forms reminded me of high school. That same mindless exercise of authority designed to beat me down hung in the air everywhere. I curled up against the tree falling into a light sleep feeling like a wild animal hiding from nearby hunters with their dogs and guns. I awoke early, my nerves worn thin and chilled to the bone.

Making my way across the field, I passed easily through the gates a few hours after daybreak. I wondered if it would be that easy to get through them on my way out. Back in the office, I slouched into one of the hard metal chairs awaiting my fate. Eventually, the sergeant came through the door to greet me. He struck that same callous stance of the indifferent bureaucrat.

"You will not be taking a physical at this time. Sign this interview acknowledgement form. We will contact you in the near future, so make sure we have your CORRECT address." He handed me another form.
Writing down my address once again, I scribbled a sloppy signature at the bottom of the page and handed him back the paper. I headed for the door thinking what a waste of time this had been coming all this way for such foolishness.

"Wait a minute!" the sergeant growled. "You didn't sign your middle initial. See your name typed in above the signature space. It includes a middle initial."

"Don't worry about that. It's no big deal. Who cares anyway," came out of me in a wise ass tone.

"All right kid but if the brass doesn't accept this signature, you will have to come back and sign it again!" he threatened.

"I'll take my chances," I said walking out the door towards the gates.

All during the trip back to Dijon my mind once again filled with thoughts of the army. What a tedious bunch of stooges. How would I ever survive all those boring bureaucrats? The more I thought about it, the more it seemed like moving backwards in time, back to the fights with teachers and authority figures during my high school days in Riverside. By the time I had returned to Dijon, my mind was made up. I would not go into the army. I didn't know exactly how things could work out, but I was sure I would not go into the army.

About a month after my interview with the sergeant, a letter came from my father. News from the induction interview had arrived at my parents' home. In his letter, my father explained that the draft board was advising me that my status for induction was being "HELD IN ABEYANCE". I had no idea what that meant and my dad wasn't too sure either. He suggested that it was some kind of bureaucratic mumbo-jumbo designed to mystify us. I looked the word up in the dictionary to discover the definition of abeyance was *a suspension in activity*. I figured as long as I stayed in France, the army would leave me alone.

Changing of the Seasons
An uneven time of year had arrived. The occasional sunny day snuck in among periods of rain and cold. By this time, my French was pretty decent. I lived life entirely immersed in the language, frequently dreaming in French. What I wanted more than anything was to be in a steady relationship with a French girl. I hoped to put my life into intimate harmony with this land that I loved. None of the French girls I had known so far stayed around long enough to qualify.

Maybe we met while we were sitting in a café or maybe where she worked at the drug store. Somehow, Sylvie

227

came into my life. She was a good natured young lady who worked in a pharmacy downtown. We began to see each other for coffee and walks. Our mutual affection grew over several weeks. Eventually, she invited me to visit her rented room for coffee and biscuits. Sylvie lived above a shop on one of the narrow streets in old town.

I found it to be a lovely room. Light flooded in through the tall paned windows. They were the old fashioned kind with mounted in two heavy frames. These swung together latching at the center of the window opening. A wash basin, mirror, and radiator pressed up against one wall. An armoire beside a simple desk and chair lined the adjacent wall. In a corner, an iron framed twin bed sat on the creaky hardwood floor. The floorboards were almost black with age; the radiator lumpy from paint on top of paint.
Sylvie did not like her place, finding it stuffy and old. I loved its cozy secluded quality in spite of the lack of modern comforts. It always thrilled me to be in the presence of objects scratched and worn by the lives of generations past.

I wondered what had happened here and if the ghosts of bygone souls still surrounded me. The old trappings of the room served as reminders of a past that seemed to burden Sylvie. She grew impatient with my speculations.
Sylvie did not live the more carefree lifestyle of young French students. The watchful eyes of Dijon society scrutinized her behavior. When we walked through town, she would look up now and again, an expression of apprehension appearing as she checked to see who might be watching us.

It took me a while to catch on. From the start, Sylvie had insisted that we stay away from the pharmacy where she worked. I did not understand why she wouldn't introduce me to her parents or invite me to her home as Félix had done. She always seemed a little nervous when we had coffee in the central square.

228

After a while, I understood that even though she treated me well and we enjoyed being together, she wanted to keep our relationship a secret from her family. Sylvie never explained why it had to be a secret. She never talked about her family. She did, however, open her life to me in other ways. She introduced Peter and me to her girlfriend, Chantal. Peter and Chantal seemed hit it off well enough.

On one of those invigorating spring days when sunlight filled the sky, the four of us went off for a picnic in Sylvie's car. We wandered through the countryside and chose a secluded little lake surrounded by woods just outside Dijon. Getting out of the car, the warm air signaled that in spite of the occasional patch of dead grass, summer was coming.

Peter got carried away in those first clear skies and warm breezes. He began to jump around in the tall grass that covered the field calling out, "Let us celebrate the wonderful truth that at our core, we're noble savages come naked into this world as good and pure a creation as any of nature's bounty. Let's take this opportunity to give ourselves back to the purity of nature."

He began taking off his clothes while declaring, "This sunny afternoon is ours to join as one with our Mother. Schools, businesses and all those man-made institutions; they've torn us away from our primal union with the earth. We can at last free ourselves of vanity and rekindle *l'amour de soi,* the goodness of our animal selves."

He pulled off his pants and threw them in the air. He began to howl like a wolf and jump around in the field. Gradually, Peter managed to take off all of his clothes. He removed each garment with great panache, swinging it around before throwing it across the field. He executed grand bows with each new piece, gesturing in the manner of a vaudeville actor.

229

None of us were as bold as Peter, but the girls got into the spirit of things. They stood across the field and took off their clothes coquettishly. With their backs to us, they waggled their behinds in our direction before putting on bathing suits. We all laughed as Peter and I cheered them on. I joined in, shedding my clothes, but stood naked only briefly before putting on my swim suit. Peter finally put on his suit.

Peter's vitality set the tone for our picnic. Sylvie smiled a lot. She seemed relaxed and happy. The girls spread a blanket and covered it with the contents of a basket including several types of cheeses, a bottle of Burgundy wine and *baguettes* of freshly baked French bread. We broke the bread into pieces with roguish gestures, drank wine by pressing the bottle to our lips, munched slices of cheese bedded in chunks of bread.

All the warmth and new life was getting to Peter. He kept glancing over at Chantal as he teased in a half joking, half challenging voice, "Our spirits roam these woods. It's up to us to follow their free will, to let our inner light guide us, to re-discover our origins. I am ready to gladly yield to the noble savage within. Are you?" He winked mischievously at Sylvie's pretty friend, tore off another piece of bread with his teeth, slugged down more wine.

Our hunger satisfied, the four of us lay back absorbing the sun. I drew close to Sylvie until our skin touched, taking in the smell of tanning oil that mixed with the nectar of her baking flesh. Grass poked its scratchy blades around my ankles and the sun's rays warmed my body.

A peaceful silence settled over the group. That afternoon, I experienced a great joy at just being alive. My entire being felt weightless and timeless, calm. That brief moment, in all its simplicity, seemed perfect. I thought to myself that it didn't matter if my life ended tomorrow. I felt these few minutes of pure joy at being alive were God's gift to me. Even after returning to our daily routine, the picnic brought Sylvie and I closer together. In spite of this growing intimacy between us, she remained unwilling to bring me into the world of her family. We continued to meet in back street cafés or in her room.

One Friday evening, when Sylvie's family left Dijon for a few days, she stayed behind. She invited Chantal, Peter, and I to spend the weekend at her family home. They lived only a few kilometers outside of Dijon.

The house had some features in common with the Devant's place, but it was set back in a wooded clearing. Enclosed by a tall brick wall, the entrance was blocked with an iron gate. Beyond the gate, the courtyard and two story stone building looked a few hundred years old, not that old by French standards, yet the house had been completely re-modeled inside. Its carpeted floors and plush furniture invited us to enjoy the comfort.

Arriving late in the afternoon, we brought supplies of food into the house. The girls shuffled utensils around the kitchen and began to work their magic. Peter and I contributed by setting the table in the dining area, knowing that another wonderful dinner would be created. We understood that we would just be in the way in the kitchen and did not attempt to interfere with the experts. We withdrew to the living room settling into stuffed chairs enjoying a view of the rustic landscape beyond the country doors.

This panoramic view of trees and woodlands inspired Peter to launch into more rumination on the joys of the natural world. He said something about nature's gift of love and finding the threads that wove us into the landscape beyond the windows. It didn't make too much sense to me, but he sounded great.

At one point, he exclaimed in a loud voice, making sure Chantal could hear, that she possessed the beauty of an Etruscan goddess. He smiled over at me. I smiled back. I thought Sylvie was wonderful. At last, I had entered her world. Enjoying this quiet evening together with friends, what could be better?

After a lovely meal, we sat around the living room talking for a time. Eventually, the conversation became spotty. Calling it a night, we headed upstairs to the bedrooms. Sylvie led me to her childhood room. In one corner, dolls clustered on a small rocking chair. The yellow painted walls were decorated with frilly white wallpaper borders. Against one wall stood a small white bed covered with a pink and white comforter, its surface a quilted pattern of brightly colored umbrellas.

The room made me uncomfortable. Sylvie told me that she wanted to make love in her childhood bed. For some time now, I had hoped for this moment when we would first make love. Yet, I felt uncomfortable at the thought of engaging in such adult pleasures while in a young girl's world. We lay on the bed wrapping ourselves together under the covers. At the end of our passionate embrace, she became melancholy as she talked about her childhood, vanished forever.

That such a heavy hearted mood could directly follow our love making confused me. How should I behave? Sylvie's sadness felt more uncomfortable than the room. I didn't want to disturb her reminiscing. I understood the heavy heartedness and wanted to comfort her. Not knowing exactly what to say, I just held her in my arms.
She was so focused on her own experience of loss that she did not notice my discomfort. It occurred to me that I had simply served as the vessel to carry her across a very personal threshold into a new stage of her life experience. I

232

felt that it was not me to whom she was making love that night, but some symbolic male whose sole purpose was to facilitate her journey. As we lay together, I felt our separateness.

The experience left me doubtful of the nature of our relationship. What had we just done and what was I to Sylvie? A void existed between us. I felt that I did not truly belong in her world.

For the first time, I grasped, at a gut level, that my life in this country had boundaries. To be French wasn't like being American. People of different religions and cultures could blend into American society. I realized that while my newly developed ability to speak and understand French had brought me this far, while it had provided me with the communication skills necessary to get close to Sylvie, it also had limitations. Speaking the language did not gain me full entry into French society. Even though I could participate in many of the wonderful experiences France had to offer, others remained beyond my reach, reserved for those born and raised here. Laying still in the dark of that child's room, I came to fully comprehend that I would never be French.

The Essence of Springtime
The next morning, Sylvie, Chantal, Peter and I bounced down the tree lined road that spring morning in her little Citroen. Everyone bustled with anticipation as we rolled toward a country breakfast at a rural inn that Sylvie had described to us. We arrived late in the morning at a picture book manor.

The two story white building set in a lush green valley gave the appearance more of a private residence than a restaurant. We chose to sit on the terrace in white wooden chairs at a table that overlooked the green pastures. New born birds chirped for food in surrounding trees, sheep grazed on a nearby hillside, their bells leisurely echoing over the fields. I occasionally caught the hollow sound of cooing pheasants. The crisp morning air filled my lungs. Another of those moments was beginning to develop when

I felt completely at peace in the world. Even the flies circling my omelet seemed to have the right to be there. With exams coming up soon, I keep thinking about Sartre's works of existentialism. I decided to ask Peter about them. "Say, Peter, I keep turning the words over in my head, but they won't stay together. Do you know what Sartre means by *essence precedes existence*? Sartre seems like such a dreary guy. I don't get it."

"It's just a bunch of words, Rich. Look at it this way. Sylvie is beautiful to you right?" He continued without waiting for a reply, "The sheep in the field, this coffee, you are free, my friend, to assign meaning to all of it. Forget about your parent's advice. There is no why. Make of this morning what you will, what you can. We are all creating and re-creating with every new moment. Invent your world. Remember, it's not healthy to swallow too many books without chewing," Peter smiled.

I sipped the coffee; it tasted wonderful. I looked at Sylvie who radiated beauty in the morning sun. Peter leaned back in his chair relaxing his arms behind his head, taking in the rays. In the fresh morning air, a bright sun slowly warmed my skin through my shirt. I could smell freshly cut grass. The crisp odor of fried eggs and recently brewed coffee drifted from the table.

If this world existed purely as a product of my invention, I knew it would be burnt into my memory forever. This gentle place in which I could mingle my very essence and blend into the surroundings felt deeply liberating. If I had somehow concocted this world, I wanted to keep it as a part of me, to re-create it. Was it actually possible to preserve the spirit of this moment, this unique universe of my own invention?

Pulling a blanket of stillness over me, I let go and tried to become a part of everything around me. My mind wondered through the fields as I listened to the sound of sheep bells, the voices of my friends. With eyes still closed, I felt myself drift off, into Sylvie's back yard, to her lawn under the dense cherry tree that I lay beneath just before we left the house that morning. I could still see the bright red cherries and the shamrock green leaves scattering the blinding rays of sunlight that burst between them. I could feel the sun pushing my eyelids shut just as it had done earlier that morning. Inventing my world, yes, that sounded like a wonderful idea. I would invent my way through the exams and on into the future.

A Day of Reckoning

The moment of judgment finally came. A lot was expected of university students in France. So different from the American system of education, the absence of regular homework assignments or quizzes left students with no way to periodically evaluate their progress. Everything depended on self-discipline.

An all-or-nothing week of exams determined success or failure. Each day of finals week began with four hours of written exams followed by four hours of oral grilling by the professors. Every new day was dedicated to a single course until the entire curriculum had been covered. That barrage of tests resulted in a passing or failing grade in each class as well as an overall score. The foreign studies were subjected to a modified version of this process while keeping the basic approach. It remained intimidating. If I had learned nothing else that year, I had learned self-discipline. Throughout that second year, I created weekly schedules working diligently to maintain them. I had paced myself to meet the challenge of final exams. I was ready.

Another difference in French exams was the emphasis on writing rather than multiple-choice questions or repeating a lot of facts. Each day of exams, I labored over a different subject writing short essays in French without the help of a dictionary. My greatest strength was showcased in responses to questions during the oral exams where my ability to speak fluent French paid off.

In the end, I barely passed most of the subjects, struggling mightily only to fall short of the mark in others. I wound up not receiving a high enough cumulative score. My grade came close, falling only a few points short of passing. Considering that less than half of those who took the tests would succeed, I felt proud of my effort. It was a personal triumph that left me with a sense of achievement in this not-so-modest accomplishment.

But for me, a curious transformation had taken place throughout the year. All that reading of French literature and studying French grammar had a side effect. Two years earlier, I could barely write in English, let alone French. By the end of that year, a significant improvement surfaced in letters to my parents. I wrote complete sentences, spelling words correctly most of the time.

The week after exams, students began rapidly disappearing from Dijon. Peter headed back to Berlin with a simple goodbye and little fanfare. Sylvie and I parted ways easily. She had probably foreseen from the outset that our lives would take different paths. Dawn, with whom I had remained friends throughout the year, moved to London. I had always admired her sense of adventure and indomitable spirit. I sensed that our paths would cross again. The dorms transformed from places of life into empty warehouses. A few days later, the student cafeteria closed its doors. It was time to move on.

I had purchased a cheap plane ticket from a student charter company with what money I had left. The flight to New York City made a stop in Reykjavik, Iceland. This would be the first time I had ever set foot on an airplane. Although my friend Sue had returned to New York City the previous year, we had remained in touch over the year. In early spring, she offered to arrange for me to sublet a flat from a friend of hers for a few months during school vacation on Manhattan's lower east side. I could work in the city for a while to raise enough money for the return trip to California. I told my parents only that I would show up at their door one day that summer

CHAPTER SEVEN
No Place Like Home

New York: The Apple's Worm

Lifting off the runway at Orly Airport in Paris went smoothly enough. Once over the ocean, however, the plane began to bounce around in the sky. It suddenly dropped like a brick for what seemed like an eternity. Finally the plane slammed to a brief recovery only to bob up and down again. The ride continued to go back and forth between smooth and rough skies. This was an older plane, a four propeller craft, equipped with thick, wax-paper lined, vomit bags that I kept ready whenever we flew into new turbulence. For a charter flight, there were not many young people on board. I didn't talk to anyone, my mind too preoccupied with images of our crash landing or plunge to the bottom of the sea.

We stayed in Reykjavik only long enough to refuel. When the stewardess opened the cabin door, gusts of ice cold air rushed in. By this time, I didn't especially feel like disembarking anyway.

New York City had always struck me as an intimidating place. Having spent much of my youth in the country, big cities never appealed to me. I disliked going to Paris after the first visit. New York was worse. So many people crowded on top of each other. Struggling through the hordes, pushing along the sidewalks, the foul air and chaotic noises left me feeling irrelevant. I gradually vanished into insignificance. Dawn had once described London as a city where, if she were ever to die alone in one of its cold-water flats, no one would discover her for years. Walking around New York, looking at all those indifferent faces, I could see what she meant.

Finally reaching Sue's place, I found her in good spirits. She hadn't changed at all, spending every free minute with her head buried in a book. While riding in cars or on the

240

subway, even while at the beach, she never looked up from her book. It was as if ideas mattered more than everyday life. As oblivious as she seemed to her immediate surrounds, her hypnotic power to focus always captured me. Just as the day I first met her in Dijon, whenever she spoke to me, only the two of us existed and the topic at hand became vitally important.

She was attending New York University while working as a waitress. Sue had gotten involved with a group on campus called 'Students for a Democratic Society'. She dedicated what little free time she had available to do volunteer work for them. Her enthusiastic participation in SDS brought to mind her interest in the French Trotsky group some eighteen months earlier in Dijon.

Sue's friend, who was leaving the city for the summer, sublet a small flat to me for a few months on First Street just off the Bowery. The first thing I notice about the flat was the door. A reinforced steel groove half way up in the center of the door matched a similar metal plate embedded in the floor. Once the associated iron bar was placed between the two and the three locks secured, nobody could break in. Bars on the windows sealed access from that direction as well. I had moved into a war zone.

Once inside, the apartment had one advantage over most French flats. There was a bathtub. It was a one bedroom apartment and the bathtub sat in the middle of a small kitchen. All the appliances showed significant wear from usage. Chunks of enamel had worn off the tub. Throughout, pale green walls scarred with old nail holes and dirty hand marks did little to inspire my curiosity about those who lived here in the past. A small band of cockroaches co-habited the place roaming around the bathtub rim with unconcerned confidence while I soaked inches away. Occasionally, I would knock one onto the kitchen floor with a flick of the finger.

241

My first night there, all the noise made sleep difficult. Things never got much better. The summer nights frequently hit one hundred degrees, the air thick with humidity. There was no air conditioning. Loud conversations rose for the pavement below into the early morning hours. The most disturbing noises came from howling women in nearby apartments. Some of their voices shouted in anger, others sounded more like screams of pain and fear. This woke me every night until I learned to sleep through it.

I secured a job working as a waiter on the night shift at Schrafts in Times Square. It turned out to be a fun job. I got to work with young aspiring artists and actors. The evening crowd that came in for late night coffee and desert were often famous celebrities stopping by after performing in a Broadway show. I enjoyed the atmosphere and got to know which theater stars were good tippers.

Returning to the flat every night by subway scared me more than any journey I had ever made. I feared being mugged. Seedy characters hung around the block of my flat. Drug dealers worked the schoolyard just below my window. I discovered that the bar near my subway stop was a local watering hole for pimps and hookers. The short walk to my apartment involved carefully stepping around drunks passed out on the pavement lying in filthy rags that must once have been clothing.

Life in New York City might have brought me down had it not been for my new sense of confidence and pride in my achievements. I had big plans to start community college once I returned to Riverside. If the French were right about their academic requirements being superior to those in the U.S.A., then I should have no problem with getting good grades in community college. Especially considering how close I had come to success in Dijon. And I had just traveled all the way around the world in three years. I was special.

It was early June. With good tips and the higher wages employers paid in New York, my savings were building rapidly. I would try to be home for my twenty-first birthday in July. That flight from Paris to New York took all the glamour out of air travel. I decided to hitch-hike across the country.

Completing the Circle

By this time, I had become a seasoned hitch-hiker. In other words, I was prepared to get picked up by some strange characters whose behavior could be dangerously erratic. My main objective became to avoid the really odd ones, even though flushing them out before getting in the car was next to impossible. My discomfort level elevated as I stood at the entrance to the George Washington Bridge sticking my thumb into the five lanes of traffic racing westward.

A fairly normal trucker gave me a lift across New Jersey to begin a journey that turned out to be long and, for the most part, uneventful. The highlights of the journey came first in Colorado where a pretty young lady picked me up outside of Vail and fed me a free lunch in the kitchen of a resort where she worked.

Then, there was the crazy ride across part of Nevada with a middle-aged man driving a shark-finned 1959 Chevrolet Impala. Its massive frame floated down the road, so much larger than anything I had become accustomed to in France. The driver seemed a bit drunk when I first climbed on board. The car smelled of beer.

After a few miles of riding with the windows open in the hot dessert air, the man behind the wheel offered me a beer, asking me to hand him a cold can from the back. Reaching over the seat, I pulled a large towel away from a massive cooler filled with ice and cans of beer. This made me nervous, but he was managing to drive well enough. As the miles of sand and sagebrush sailed by, the number of beer cans flying out the window grew. My driver began to weave in and out of his lane. When he stopped to refill in Mesquite, I abandoned ship to wait for a less risky ride.

Throughout the journey, all I could think about was what it would be like to return to Riverside after circling the globe. I imagined big parades and the mayor giving me the key to the city in honor of my amazing feat. All of my friends would stare at me in awe, envious of my great accomplishments. My parents would be so proud that they would brag to all the jealous neighbors of their adventuresome and intelligent son.

We rolled into Riverside from the east, taking the same route I had traveled some seven years earlier when our family moved to California from Rochester, New York. How different it felt this time. In place of that agitated youth filled with anxiety at coming west to a fearsome future, I arrived full of energy, confident, the conquering hero. As we drove through downtown, it struck me just how small and parochial Riverside appeared. We passed my old high school, a place filled with inexperienced youth, clearly inferior beings lacking any worldly sophistication.

The driver let me out at the corner of Magnolia Avenue and Roslyn Street. It was mid-afternoon on a Saturday. What lay before me was the half mile walk back to my parents house at the end of Roslyn St. I had walked down this street many times on my way home from Ramona High School. I recognized every house, every car. Nothing had changed.

It was the longest half mile of my entire journey. With each step I took, I grew more humble. No big parades, no keys to the city awaited me. Actually, the few people I saw

244

out washing their cars or working in the yard didn't pay much attention as I passed. I became acutely aware that people were busy with their own lives. They didn't know or care to hear about where I had been for the last three years.

When I finally reached our house, the front door swung back and a man opened the screen door, a tired old man with wrinkles and grey hair. The look in his eyes was a strange union of sadness and joy, of weariness and relief.

His face twisted into an unwilling half smile as if he were resisting the mix of sentiments welling up inside him. I knew that look intimately. The feelings behind it bound us together. It was his special way of trying to suppress emotions fearing he might show signs of vanity or weakness. When he shook my hand to welcome me home, I felt the callused skin of my dad's hand, his firm grip strained with emotion.

I knew that he was doing more than just shaking my hand. The last time my dad held my hand was when he took me for walks in the Tennessee hills as a young boy. This simple gesture meant a lot. The son of a Slovakian immigrant, Dad never lost that Eastern European reserve. For him, survival demanded the suppression of any sentimentality. Emotions could not be trusted in his world where science ruled supreme. A warm handshake was one of the few ways Dad allowed himself to express his love. It was, also, his way of acknowledging that I was no longer a boy, but a young man.

My mother stood behind him. I passed over the threshold, went right up to her and gave her a big hug and a kiss. This was something I had not done in so many years that I could not remember showing that much affection, even as a child. The French habit of always greeting friends with a kiss helped me. She hugged me for a long time.

245

We sat in the living room while I told them about some of
the places I had seen, the people I met, and the events that
had happened. As I sat there on the couch talking, I
glanced around occasionally to take in the surroundings.
Nothing much had been moved; the same bookcases were
filled with the same books. My grandmother's circular rag
rug covered the carpet where it had always been. Somehow, this world felt lifeless, too quiet.
I went to my room to unpack. It looked much as it had during my high school years. The desk remained prominently
positioned as I opened the door, exactly where it stood
three years before. The 1946 Zenith radio that I had picked
up in a church rummage sale in Rochester silently weighed
down one corner of the desk. Its white needle still pointed
to the rock and roll station that had inspired many a night
of wakeful dreaming. My record player and collection of
Elvis records rested in the corner where I had left them.
Picking up the wooden and brass book ends that I had
made in high school woodshop, I discovered them to be
heavier than I recalled.

Signs of change were also present. Foreign objects had
crept in during my absence. Half of the closet was filled
with my mother's clothing. Her sewing machine was
tucked away in a corner of the closet. Knitting needles
stuck out of the pencil holder.

I lay back on the bed and, even though I knew it was completely ridiculous, I felt sad, even disappointed, at the lack
of a hero's welcome. I picked up my copy of *Catcher in
the Rye* which still lay on the nightstand. Holden Caulfield
had been such a hero to me three years earlier. I could no
longer remember why I admired him so much. I noticed
the little paperback's pages were a brownish yellow.
Putting the book down, I wondered why, even though so
much remained the same, nothing felt very familiar. It finally came to me as I lay staring blankly at the ceiling. I
was the one who had changed.

Made in the USA
Middletown, DE
25 November 2020